The Health Services Continuum in Democratic States

Odin W. Anderson

The Health Services Continuum in Democratic States

An Inquiry into Solvable Problems

Health Administration Press   Ann Arbor, Michigan 1989

Library of Congress Cataloging-in-Publication Data

Anderson, Odin W. (Odin Waldemar)
    The health services continuum in democratic states : an inquiry into
solvable problems / Odin W. Anderson.
    p. cm.
    Includes index.
    ISBN 0-910701-06-7 (soft)
    1. Medical care. 2. Public health. 3. Insurance, Health. I. Title.
    [DNLM: 1. Delivery of Health Care—organization & administration.
W 84.1 A549h]
RA425.A733 1989 362.1—dc20 DNLM/DLC for Library of Congress
89-11225 CIP

Health Administration Press
A Division of the Foundation of the
  American College of Healthcare Executives
1021 East Huron Street
Ann Arbor, Michigan 48104-9990
(313) 764-1380

To my immediate family: Helen Hay Anderson, my wife since 1939, my daughter Kristin Alice, my son Thor Edwin, my daughter-in-law Jane Bowling Anderson, and my two grandchildren, Glenn Magni Anderson and Ashley Belle Anderson.

Contents

List of Tables and Figures

Foreword

Odin Anderson is the dean of scholars throughout the world who study health policy, and no one has done more to develop the field of health policy as a legitimate area of concern within universities in the United States and abroad. When he went to New York City in 1952 to become Research Director of the Health Information Foundation (HIF), the study of health policy was an underdeveloped field of research and teaching within American universities. When he left ten years later to accept the position of Research Director of the Center for Health Administration Studies and Professor of Sociology in both the Graduate School of Business and the Department of Sociology—all at the University of Chicago—the study of health policy had become a respectable field of study in a number of American universities.

The numerous studies that he sponsored and carried out at HIF during his ten years there did much to make health policy studies a highly visible area of academic research. By building on this impressive record since his arrival at the University of Chicago, he has been very much responsible for the status that health policy studies presently enjoy in universities throughout the world. The studies of health care utilization that he helped to develop at HIF and the University of Chicago are indispensable historical documents concerning the consumption of medical services. Meantime, he has trained during his career three generations of scholars in the area of health policy studies.

If his book *Health Care: Can There Be Equity? The United States,*

Sweden and England (New York: John Wiley & Sons, Inc., 1972) was not the first cross-national study of health, it was certainly the best comparative study of health care that anyone had yet produced. As a result of Anderson's pioneering work in comparative analysis, a number of other scholars in a variety of disciplines have subsequently undertaken cross-national studies of health care. However, those who want to study the history of American medical care within a comparative framework with an emphasis on organizational features, financial arrangements, utilization patterns, and personnel still find that book and other of Anderson's works necessary reading. No one has been more productive in carrying out both cross-national and within-nation studies of health care than Odin Anderson.

While he has written extensively about other countries, Anderson has throughout his career been primarily interested in the American health care system. And though the literature on medical care has often been highly emotional, his writing has never been polemical in nature. Much of his concern has been to understand why the Americans have produced such a distinctive medical system and to share his understanding with others. To this end, he has believed that it is necessary to study a medical delivery system within its political and cultural context. He has long assumed that a comparative analysis is necessary if one is to understand any single system.

In the present study, as in his other work, he assumes that each system emerges from a long history that reflects the values distinctive to each nation. Anderson believes that a nation's ability to import a system from another society is limited. Indeed, in this study, he convincingly demonstrates that the direction in which medical systems will change is very much directed by the social structure and culture from which they have emerged. Thus, Anderson makes it clear that while national medical systems have been converging in terms of much of their technology, they nevertheless vary considerably in terms of those elements shaped by their society's traditions: their organizational structures, the methods of payment for medical services, the degree of autonomy experienced by medical doctors, and the degree of access to services. His comparative perspective, in this, as in other work, has been very useful in assisting us to understand what types of problem have some potential to be solved under state sponsorship and reform, and what types of problem tend to persist irrespective of the source of funding or irrespective of whether a medical system is predominantly owned in the public, voluntary, or for-profit sector.

Most academic disciplines have become increasingly specialized in the twentieth century, and as a consequence, scholars have more and more difficulty communicating effectively with others within and across academic disciplines. Much of this difficulty has resulted from the fact that scholars have attempted to work with very few variables. In contrast, Anderson's work is broad in scope, highly interdisciplinary, and refreshing.

Anderson's study reflects a pragmatic and skeptical style. For him, every system falls far short of perfection. This book, like others of his which have preceded it, helps us to understand the strengths and weaknesses of individual systems and offers insights as to what types of incremental change are possible and may make health care more effective. This type of scholarship—the serious effort to demonstrate what we know and do not know, addressed to scholars, policy intellectuals, policymakers, and a well educated lay public—must continue if we are to maintain a public policy process influenced by an informed public and if our institutions are to function in a democratic manner.

Since 1980, Anderson has had a joint appointment, serving as Professor of Sociology at the University of Wisconsin and continuing his active involvement at the Center for Health Administration Studies of the University of Chicago. During this period, he has tirelessly commuted between both universities, completed his study *Health Services in the United States: A Growth Enterprise Since 1875,* and written this book. Since he joined the faculty of the University of Wisconsin, it has been my privilege to teach with him and learn from him. It has been a rich experience.

J. Rogers Hollingsworth
University of Wisconsin

Acknowledgments

I wish to acknowledge the Department of Sociology, University of Wisconsin–Madison, and the Center for Health Administration Studies, Graduate School of Business, University of Chicago for the congenial atmosphere these institutions provided for writing a book of this kind. They offered vast library resources, freedom from details of academic administration, and unaccounted time. Project Hope, of Millwood, Virginia, made me a Resident Scholar and provided me with funds for clerical work, research assistants, and travel to Toronto, Ottawa, and Montreal. Frank Place, a graduate student in economics, gathered a great deal of statistical background information on expenditures for health services, economic history, and economic comparisons between countries. Ronald Rodgers, a graduate student in law and industrial relations, wrote a position paper for me on the status and nature of collective bargaining and on the unionization of physicians and nurses cross-nationally. Karen Schneider, a major in Italian, translated two books on the Italian health services. All of these students were at the University of Wisconsin, Madison. Any manuscript requires tedious and painstaking typing and retyping; for this service I am grateful to Virginia Rogers, Toni Schulze, Terri Skinner, and Diana Taylor of the Department of Sociology. Finally, Nancy J. Moncrieff at Health Administration Press did a magnificent job of copyediting a complex manuscript; I will be forever in her debt.

Odin W. Anderson, Ph.D.
University of Wisconsin–Madison
and
University of Chicago

Chapter 1

Introduction

For purposes of international comparison, if the personal health services delivery systems of the United States did not exist, they would have to be invented. This country has become a convenient international reference point, not to be emulated, of the extreme of inequality and wasted resources. The U.S. health services are still envied for their widely distributed technology, first-class facilities, and accompanying specialization, but these strong points come at too high a price. Likewise, for purposes of international comparison, if the British National Health Service did not exist, it would also have to be invented. It has become a convenient international reference point of the opposite extreme, for relatively low cost, equity and fairness, primary care, and a reasonably adequate technology if a certain level of rationing and denial of service is accepted.

This book makes the ambitious attempt to synthesize the development, organization, and financing of personal health services among several industrially developed states that have liberal-democratic political and economic systems. My personal experience and direct access to the data of the liberal-democratic states limit me to those states. Among them, I have picked seven for more intensive description and analysis. But, for analytical purposes, I am less interested in the characteristics of any individual country than in generalizing over a range of countries. What is regarded as a modern, scientifically oriented, specialized health services delivery system has certain characteristics that are found all over the world, from countries in the early stages of industrial development to those that have reached industrial maturity and are entering what is now called the postindustrial stage of high technology, with the service sector exceeding the production sector. Among these characteristics is the rationalistic-reductionist, single-disease-orientation model. My choice of countries is intended not to ignore the seeming countermoves of holistic medicine in developed countries but to recognize that the rationalistic-reductionist-model countries continue to dominate the world.

Why embark on this kind of comparative enterprise? What is the scientific and health policy justification for it? Quite a few years ago when I began to engage in research, I quite naturally started with the health care delivery systems in the United States. (Systems are plural here because there are a variety of health care delivery systems in this country, ranging from closed-panel groups and salaried physician prepayment plans to the open, fee-for-service, more or less individual practice arrangements and health insurance companies. Fee-for-service, individual medical practice and voluntary hospitals continue to be the mainstream of American health care delivery although, of course, the situation is changing, and the future shape of our systems is not clear.) As I moved into research on the utilization and expenditure patterns in this country, I noted quite a bit of variability by region of the country and by type of delivery system. Further, I began to assemble data on utilization and expenditure patterns from other countries that included such information in their official reports—Canada, the United Kingdom, and Sweden.

I found that hospital admissions ranged from 200 per 1,000 population in the province of Saskatchewan to 85 per 1,000 in the United Kingdom, with the United States and Sweden somewhere between. I noted also a remarkable difference in the average length of a hospital stay—8 days in Saskatchewan, similar to the United States, but 12 to 15 days in the United Kingdom and in Sweden. Physician visits per person also varied from three or so per year in Sweden to four or five in the United States and the United Kingdom.

Total health care expenditures in these countries varied from 4 percent to 8 percent of the gross national product (GNP), with the United Kingdom having the lowest percentage and the United States the highest, although Canada and Sweden were hardly on the low side. The United Kingdom was and continues to be unique in its relatively low level of expenditure as measured by percentage of GNP. These countries were not remarkably different in their industrial development and standard of living, and they all are democracies which implies that public policy decisions, including those for health services, are formulated largely through a pluralistic, interest-group process (with some interest groups, of course, being more influential than others).

My obvious conclusion was that no single health services delivery system, even if it were one of several within a given country as in the United States, could be its own reference point in the sense that the temperature of a normal human body is 98.6 degrees Fahrenheit. There is no delivery system that can be standardized, like a life insurance company or an automobile manufacturing company, and be applicable anywhere in the world, or even anywhere in the world that there are resources and trained managers and personnel. It was startling to realize that personal health care systems have in substance no performance indicators as to input and output—hence the variations I found in my preliminary comparisons.

That there are no indicators appears to be a simplistic and arbitrary conclusion, as well as a frustrating one for health services managers and physicians. Each delivery system does in fact have internal equilibrium points more or less peculiar to it, depending on the relative balances between the interest groups within the system. The major equilibrium points, in no particular order, are: (1) the public and private expenditures and effective demand; (2) the personnel, particularly physicians; (3) the hospitals and their managers; (4) the sources of funding, private or public; (5) the relative financial resources of the country, and (6) the morbidity and mortality patterns. When I say there are no performance indicators to assist policymakers in fashioning a rational health services delivery system, I am referring to current indicators such as utilization and expenditure patterns, ratios of facilities and personnel to population, and mortality and disease patterns, with mortality and disease patterns presumed to be the ultimate outcome measures used to justify expenditures for personal health services.

Since no health services delivery system can be its own reference point, one must use the usual methodology of social science, and indeed of comparative anatomy, to investigate how more or less similar systems operate in more or less similar circumstances. The researcher must collect data and make observations. Among the various conditions for health services delivery, what are the extreme ranges of utilization and expenditure patterns? What are the extreme ranges of number of hospital beds and physicians to population? What are the sources of capital? What is the process of policy formation; that is, how do political pressure groups function? What are regarded as salient health and political issues? What are the variations in organized patterns of delivery? Based on these considerations, is it possible to determine the intrinsic and generic nature of a modern health services delivery system? What are the apparent differences? To what extent does it seem possible to manage and direct a personal health services delivery system? Is it essentially unmanageable, like a big river that flows along inexorably, directed only here and there for flood control or irrigation? This analogy does not seem too far-fetched when one observes the universality of disease, pain, and premature death and populations' persistent demand for cure, relief, and assurance. In all countries, a health services system has been the response: a remarkable, complex, and costly edifice.

International comparisons of health services systems in any depth are made exceedingly difficult by the relative lack of statistical data of facilities, of personnel and their types, of expenditure patterns, or even of a national aggregate nature, although for the latter such data are better than for other elements.[1] There are differences in definitions of hospitals, physicians, nurses, and expenditure categories.[2] I believe it is reasonable, however, to presume that these differences in definition are not so serious that one cannot arrive at some valid generalizations. It is at the micro level of description and analysis that these definitional differences become serious. I hope that the macro level of abstraction here will establish a framework for future scholars. To them will fall the more onerous task of gathering primary, micro-level data, of going beyond the precollected data assembled for policy and administrative purposes rather than for research and analytical ones. All of the information and data I present in this book are drawn from already existing data collected and assembled for other purposes than mine. I do attempt a synthesis of existing data sources in Chapters 9, 10, and 11.

The relative softness of cross-national data at a point in time can be mitigated by drawing on long-term trend data on the assumption that countries have not in substance changed their definitions and categories much over time. Trend data may be much more significant for comparison of countries than data at a point in time. Are the trend indicators in the same direction but different in pace? Are the same forces operating similarly in all countries? Even cursory observations of trends indicate that the health services enterprises in all developed and developing countries have grown since the emergence of scientific medicine in the latter nineteenth century in Europe and in North America and that that growth has accelerated geometrically during the last 30 years.

The most astonishing observation may be that, regardless of country, scientific medicine seems to have created similar types of health services, facilities, and personnel. General and long-term hospitals are more or less the same in all countries and seem to the cross-national observer to repeat themselves. The same is true for physicians, although countries may have different proportions of general or family practitioners and different mixes of specialists, and for nurses, dentists, pharmacists, and technicians of various kinds. The major differences are in the ownership of facilities, the arrangements for contracting services with physicians and pharmacists, the sources of capital funding, the sources of funding for daily operation, the manner in which the facilities and personnel are related to each other, the method for reimbursing facilities and personnel for services, the relative proportions of private and public sources of funding, and the extent to which access to services is regarded as a universal right.

The similarity in types of facilities and personnel appears to be a result of the medical technological imperative. This is to say that the application of the scientific method to healing resulted in the rationalistic-reductive orientation of modern medicine generally, and this in turn created the various medical specialists and the technical infrastructure of the modern hospital. The physician through legal monopoly acquired the right to diagnose and treat within the wide, discretionary range of formally and informally established professional norms. The nurse acquired more and more technical skills so that the whole patient became fragmented into body parts and disease. I do not mean to imply, however, that the pre-rationalistic-reductionist health services practices were overwhelmingly effective.

Before the last quarter of the nineteenth century, there were many practicing physicians drawing on medical lore and empirical medicine. Hospitals, however, were mostly used for the destitute sick and as storehouses for a social underclass; they bore no resemblance to modern hospitals. Nor did those called nurses bear any resemblance to modern nurses and technicians. With the discovery of antisepsis and anesthetics, surgery became relatively safe and painless. Already existing surgical experience and skills were rather quickly applicable on a mass basis in the hospitals. In due course, medical patients followed surgical patients, and somewhat later births increasingly took place in hospitals.

The transformation of personal health services followed technologically the transformation of the economic system from agriculture to industry. The personal health services became the recipients of the social surpluses that were growing beyond basic food, clothing, and shelter for the increasing capital and operating requirements of a voracious human needs enterprise. In the industrialized world, personal health services have been a growth enterprise since the latter nineteenth century. This growth caused no concern until after the rapid acceleration following World War II and especially after 1970.

In all industrialized countries in the liberal-democratic orbit there was thus an opportunity for personal health services to evolve in relation to the expanding economy, the general industrial technological revolution, and the relatively leisurely pace of the liberal-democratic political process. The costs of personal health services did not become a serious political issue in Europe until the turn of the century. Although Germany under Otto von Bismarck embarked on government health insurance for the working class as early as 1883, the structure of personal health services appeared to evolve more slowly, shaped largely by the medical establishment and private and public patrons.

The liberal-democratic political and economic framework sanctioned the creation of agencies quite independent of the state, following the demise of the mercantile system and the guild system after the European middle-class revolutions. Political and economic pluralism created several power centers; political and economic interest groups debated public policy and legislation in parliamentary structures. For over a hundred years, the franchise was gradually extended to all adults above a certain age regardless of sex or social class. The European and North American personal health services enterprises were a product of the emerging and middle-class professional groups and business enterprises operating both through the state and through voluntary agencies independent of the state. With some risk of oversimplification, it can be stated that the personal health services in Europe and North America were started mostly by private initiative, aided and abetted by government support and legislation. The ultimate custodian of the public interest was the liberal-democratic government, created to blunt the original power of the aristocracy and the monarchy and legitimated through popular elections. Even so, "government" became more or less an interest group whose grasp for power was just as self-seeking as that of any other interest group. The United States is regarded as the country whose traditional political philosophy within the liberal-democratic orbit has been chary of centralized power even through elected representatives, and possibly Sweden stands at the other extreme. The philosophy of government's counterbalancing private-sector interest groups affects the structure, financing, and equity of the health services.

The seemingly leisurely development of the personal health services infrastructure among the liberal-democratic governments from the latter part of the nineteenth century to the present time stemmed from the incremental policy-making nature of the liberal-democratic political and economic philosophy. Also, once some of the technical advances of scientifically and empirically based medicine became obvious to the public, the medical establishment and the general hospitals found a steadily expanding demand for services—bought privately by the public or subsidized by the government through one form of tax or other, such as payroll deduction or a consumption or general revenue tax. Many general hospitals were transformations of hospitals owned by religious bodies. Philanthropic funding agencies and wealthy individuals established nonsectarian hospitals, notably in England, the Commonwealth countries, and the United States. Central and local governments built hospitals largely for the poor, although the privately sponsored hospitals also served a large "deserving poor" clientele.

In all countries in the liberal-democratic orbit during the latter nineteenth century and continuing along with industrial maturity, the personal health services infrastructure seemed to evolve through three quite similar stages. The first stage was the development of the health services infrastructure. This stage in all liberal-democratic countries began during the last quarter of the nineteenth century and reached a plateau by the 1930s. The general hospital, the physician and the specialist, the nurse, the dentist, and the pharmacist had evolved into types and in their relative professional differentiation from each other. Each entity had its own professional domain, with the exception of the nurse (after the private duty nurse was phased out), and each had its expenditure category leading to fiscal differentiation from both private and public sources. In European countries, by and large, physicians split into those who became specialists in hospitals and those who became generalists and family practitioners outside of hospitals. In North American and the Commonwealth countries, physicians mostly became entrepreneurs outside of hospitals; they maintained their own offices and made arrangements with hospitals for admitting privileges. This differentiation is not as pure now as it once was, but it remains a major contrast to the European pattern; the reasons for this differentiation are fortuitous and historical rather than intrinsic and medical organizational. By the 1930s all developed countries had evolved quite parallel personal health services infrastructures as to type of personnel and facilities, seemingly independent of sources of capital funds and daily operating expenditures; they were products of the same medical technological forces.

Stage two was the development of the third party to pay for the daily operating expenditures of the personal health services. This came about through some form of health insurance, either public or private. The third party was to relieve the burden of at least high-cost medical episodes to economically vulnerable segments of the population. Low-income workers (the worthy poor, who in Europe constituted probably 80 percent of the population) came under some kind of private or public health insurance. The third party was grafted onto the existing health services delivery structure with no thought of changing it. The structure was a given. In most of these countries, stages one and two overlapped, although in North America these stages were quite distinct. In any case, in most countries the third party began to emerge with some magnitude and pace after, say, World War I in the form of universal health insurance coverage. By the 1950s, the third party development had run its course to universality in all countries except the United States, Canada, Australia, and South Africa. In these countries there emerged quite vigorous third parties in private health insurance coverage that appeared to slow the drive to universality; but in 1968 Canadian health insurance became universal.

Stage three is the management and control of the health services infrastructure, driven by the desire to contain and slow the rapidly rising cost to both the private and public sectors, the major funding sources. This stage, which all countries are now experiencing, expresses itself in budget controls on the infrastructure and in planning according to a presumed rational model. There was no directed planning of the volume of supply or funding until recently; the process was incremental since no body of planners could actually envision future developments and make rational calculations balancing need, demand, and appropriate expenditures. Indeed, uncertainty continues to bedevil those who wish to manage and control the health services infrastructures of developed countries. No matter who owns the facilities, how the physicians are paid, and how universal the insurance coverage, all countries are agonizing over how to manage and control.

In addition to problems of definitions and statistics, a far more important problem underlying international comparisons is that of identifying similarities and dissimilarities and determining what they mean. As Jerzy Wiatr states, similarities and dissimilarities depend on how one interprets data cross-nationally.[3] One must have a theoretical and empirical knowledge of relationships in general. In making observations of health services delivery systems, I have noted that physicians, hospital managers, nurses, dentists, and pharmacists relate to each other in quite similar ways and that differences are a matter of degree. The physician everywhere has a great deal of freedom to diagnose and treat; a tremendous latent and actual demand for personal health services, stemming from morbidity patterns and perceptions of ill-health, exists everywhere. Almost all seeking of care is patient-initiated, and health services delivery systems everywhere try to respond to demand. Among the dissimilarities, it appears that two dominant types of political-economic system—one liberal-democratic and pluralistic and the other socialistic—generate different organizational and financing structures. As expressed by Mark Field, one type of system is largely a demand model, the other a command model.[4] The demand model characterizes the health services in liberal-democratic countries so far.

On a more global basis, Karl Deutsch and others conceptualize politics and government as a hierarchy of four steering systems.[5] The biggest and most inaccurate (Deutsch's term) of these systems is society itself. Despite its complexity, society steers itself to some degree, in the sense that "life goes on" even after major disturbances. (In this connection I remember an observation made by the eminent sociologist at the University of Wisconsin, E. A. Ross, during the 1930s: "Society is tough.") Deutsch and his colleagues observe that a smaller and less inaccurate steering system is that of politics, involving all the formal and informal processes of allocation and decision making. A still smaller and more discernable level in the hierarchy of steering systems is the state, with its bureaucracy, laws, courts, policy, and military establishments. Finally, there is the government, "as an instrument of fine tuning in day-to-day affairs."

It seems reasonable to assume that these four steering systems are interrelated in ways difficult to elucidate qualitatively and quantitatively. For health services delivery systems, there emerge on the societal level the concept of equality, the perception of ill health, and the nurturing function of the family expressed through structured health services delivery systems. Through the overall regulatory agency of the state comes the framework through which health services are conceptualized and made available in some way. Through the political system various interest groups push for their concerns, ranging from the cost of doing research on dread diseases to the ways in which health services are conceptualized. The government assumes the responsibility of the daily operation of the health services.

I can hardly promise an explicit application of this hierarchy of steering systems to cross-national comparisons of health service delivery systems, but its concepts can serve as a loose framework. I find Carl Friedrich's concept of level of explanation plausible not only to justify my necessary level of abstraction, but to put the quantitative-qualitative problem in some perspective.[6] Friedrich asserts that in many areas of inquiry into the political process (in this case, the emergence and operation of health services delivery systems), central phenomena are in essence not quantifiable and may not even be the central phenomena. I do not expect to prove anything in a traditional, scientific, experimental way, but I hope to make sense of why certain events and configurations take place over a range of cases. As Friedrich states, "'proving' in such fields as politics and medicine typically means making more probable and hence the logic of probability judgments is essential to scientific proof here.[7]

There have been attempts to construct a typology of health services delivery systems for analytical purposes, but, although helpful, these are rather crude. I do not claim that the typology I adopt will achieve a much higher level of sophistication, but I hope that it will be useful enough for the purpose. More sophisticated typologies will have to wait for more data to show the complex internal interrelationships of health services delivery systems, the internal power relationships of political systems in the formulation of public policy, and the overarching social systems from which emanate the values of individual and public responsibility and distributive justice and the concept of a desirable standard of living. Social systems are not easily malleable according to some concept of achieving the desirable by directed planning. Even highly centralized command systems must eventually cope with intransigent elements in human nature, and other systems liberate the individual to the point where there may be a frustration of choice.

Milton Roemer has observed firsthand the health services delivery systems of more countries, both developed and developing, in both liberal-democratic and socialist political systems, than any other authority in health services organizations (and there are 40 or more of these organizations). He has contributed greatly to opening up the field of cross-national research, usually limiting himself to the organizational and financial patterns at a given time, although paying some attention to the historical forces shaping the systems. In one article he classifies health services programs into four types: (1) free enterprise, (2) social insurance, (3) public assistance, and (4) universal service.[8] In another classification, he names five categories: (1) free enterprise, (2) welfare state, (3) underdeveloped, (4) transitional, and (5) socialist.[9] These categories are not mutually exclusive.

Mark Field makes probably a tighter classification of health services programs by conceptualizing rather pure types for analytical purposes: (1) private, (2) a pluralistic mixture of public and private, (3) insurance, (4) social security, (5) national health service, and (6) socialized.[10] These categories are not mutually exclusive.

J. H. Babson has defined categories loosely, by clusters of countries and their characteristic organizational patterns: (1) Scandinavia, with considerable local autonomy in a governmental system; (2) Central Europe, where the provincial governments are responsible for hospital service; and (3) Latin America, which combines diverse ownership with complex national administrative controls.[11]

An exceedingly ambitious attempt at international comparisons is the study Robert Kohn and Kerr White and staff conducted and edited from 1967 to 1974.[12] The major feature of this study was the collection of data on use of services through a household survey of 48,000 respondents representing 15 million people in 12 study areas in seven countries. The objective was to determine the volume of use of personal health services in relation to the form of the health services delivery systems, the stock of hospitals and personnel, and many other factors. Recognizing the difficulties of relating the many variables, one of the summary statements says, "The intent at this point is not so much to present relationships as to present comparisons, to estimate differences in emphasis, and to note patterns."[13] The authors wisely concluded that there is no single factor or combination of factors that can at this time explain all the variations in use of health services. They anticipated this, given the very diverse cultural values, political systems, and organizational arrangements in the seven countries of the 12 study areas.

My own typology which I started to use in my book *Health Care: Can There Be Equity?* is based on a decision-making continuum with decentralized and centralized as the ends.[14] The continuum shows the degree to which control over funding both for capital and operating expenditures is pluralistic or centralized. Central aspects of this continuum are the relative proportions of funding that come from public or private sources and the extent to which there are parallel public or privately owned delivery systems, since, in the liberal-democratic countries, there is some degree of ambiguity as to the respective roles and obligations of government and of private enterprise for the provision of health services. Chapter 2 will elaborate on this continuum.

Notes

1. Lola Jean Kozak, Ronald Andersen, and Odin W. Anderson, *The Status of Hospital Discharge Data in Six Countries*. U.S. Department of Health, Education and Welfare. National Center for Health Statistics. Data Evaluation and Methods Research, no. 80, March 1980.
2. Robert J. Maxwell, *Health and Wealth: An International Study of Healthcare Spending* (Lexington, MA: Lexington Books, 1981).
3. Jerzy Wiatr, "The Role of Theory in the Process of Cross-National Research," in *Cross-National Comparative Survey Research: Theory and Practice,* ed. Alexander Szalai and Riccardo Petrella (Oxford: Pergamon Press, 1977), pp. 347–72.
4. Mark G. Field, "Comparative Health Systems: Differentiation and Convergence; Final Report," unpublished paper, prepared for the National Center for Health Services, Rockville, MD, n.d.
5. Karl W. Deutsch, Jorge I. Domínguez, Hugh Eclo, et al. *Comparative Government Politics of Industrialized and Developed Countries* (Boston: Houghton Mifflin, 1981), p. 3.
6. Carl J. Friedrich, "Some General Theoretical Reflections on the Problems of Political Data," in *Comparing Nations: The Use of Quantitative Data in Cross-National Research,* ed. Richard L. Merritt and Stein Rokkan (New Haven, CT: Yale University Press, 1966), pp. 57–72.
7. Ibid., p. 61.
8. Milton I. Roemer, "A Classification of Medical Care Systems in Relation to Public Health Organization," in *Health Care Systems in World Perspective* (Ann Arbor, MI: Health Administration Press, 1976), pp. 251–56.
9. Milton I. Roemer, *Comparative National Policies on Health Care* (New York: Marcel Dekker, 1977), pp. 21–22.
10. Field, "Comparative Health Systems."
11. J. H. Babson, *Health Care Delivery: A Multi-National Survey* (London: Pitman Medical Press, 1972), p. 4.
12. Robert Kohn and Kerr L. White, *Health Care: An International Study, Report of the World Health Organization/International Collaborative Study of Medical Care Utilization* (London: Oxford University Press, 1976).
13. Ibid., p. 352.
14. Odin W. Anderson, *Health Care: Can There be Equity? The United States, Sweden and England* (New York: John Wiley & Sons, 1972). An interim article of mine began to form the basis for this book before I had delved deeply into the health delivery systems of many countries outside of the three named. "Are National Health Services Systems Converging? Predictions for the United States," *Annals of the American Association of Political and Social Science,* 434 (November 1977): 24–38.

Chapter 2

The Framework

More than previous typologies of health services delivery systems, the framework presented here emphasizes the political process in the systems' development. The framework is a relatively simple and graphic method to present the liberal-democratic model of both political entity and health care delivery system. To understand how the continuum describes health care delivery systems, one must first understand how it describes political entities.

All states selected for case study here—the United Kingdom, Sweden, Canada, West Germany (the Federal Republic of Germany), France, Australia, and the United States—belong in the liberal-democratic range of economic and political systems and can be placed in a continuum, a graphic illustration of which is attempted in Figure 1.

At the left end of the continuum are the countries whose political and economic systems I call market-minimized. At the right end of the continuum are the countries whose systems I call market-maximized. In this model, the fundamental political values remain constant over time and from country to country while the role of the government varies.

The constant political values are support for the following:

1. The sovereignty of the people legitimated in open elections of candidates at regular intervals. Winners become the law-making body of society within constitutional limits.

2. A judiciary independent of the executive and legislative branches of the government.

3. A government of laws and not of people. The consequences of specified acts are predictable within the framework of law.

4. The assurance that a person may not be deprived of life, liberty, or property without due process of law; the right of petition and redress of grievances through the courts; and freedom of speech, assembly, and association.

The role of the government varies with respect to the production and distribution of goods and services.

This continuum builds on Gerard DeGré's concept and has remained essentially unchanged from the middle of the nineteenth century to the present.[1] It describes liberal, parliamentary democracies that have historically developed strong private economic sectors, with government playing an indirect role in facilitation and regulation but with little government ownership of the means of production and distribution.

As the entrepreneurial and professional middle and upper-middle classes emerged in these countries and proved their technical and managerial skills, they created a social surplus that spilled over into endeavors such as education, health services, the arts, and warring for national honor and commercial expansion.[2] Decade by decade from the latter nineteenth century in Europe and North America, national wealth increased 10 percent to 15 percent with only occasional dips during depressions. Enough surplus

Figure 1: The Market-Minimized/Market-Maximized Continuum

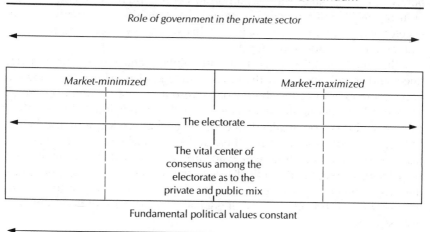

wealth was generated for reinvestment in the economies and the health services, and medical technology became more elaborate and more expensive.

As the philosophy of the role of the state emerged, it tended toward laissez faire: it limited government to the maintenance of law and order, adjudication of disputes, and control of the military and currency, leaving the means of production and distribution to private ownership. The assumption was, and is, that laissez faire would result in both a rational political process and a rational economic process. Rationality was attained in the political system through open debate and popular vote and in the economic system through the private market mechanism.[3]

Laissez faire relies on pluralism—a mix of private and public functions and responsibilities. Pluralism in turn relies on checks and balances, with more or less diffusion of the power centers and with political pressure groups in constant tension.[4] Pluralism occupies a middle ground between anarchy and totalitarianism. Its political system is sufficiently open (although some see it as not open enough) that individuals or groups can find a niche for their efforts, abilities, and aspirations in some politically tolerable relationship to one another and within legitimate rules.

Tension is inherent in all social systems, but the liberal-democratic pluralistic system is revolutionary in that the government becomes more or less another interest group in cooperation, competition, and negotiation with individuals and groups. Compared with previous societies and some contemporary societies, liberal-democratic states afford individuals great latitude in which to maneuver and work in a sense that feudal and contemporary one-party states do not purport to permit. There is, of course, criticism of the liberal-democratic systems: that they do not actually operate according to even an approximation of this theory. It would seem, however, that the theory is operating in substance.

Inevitably in all systems there are winners and losers, however defined, and equally inevitably the losers wish to minimize losses by using the government to enforce the sharing of the resources that are produced, so as to establish an economic floor below which no individual should fall—essentially this is a politically defined level, evoking concepts of distributive justice. Inevitably also, it seems, there are winners who win all the time and losers who lose all the time, which according to Marxist theory creates and perpetuates a social and political system that is deficient to the extent that there are segments in society unable to take part adequately in the system because of their poverty or lack of education or because of discrimination against them.

The question stands, however, as to what a political system does to give power to the powerless. Fundamentally, it would seem that unless a society subscribes to the moral position that it will adequately assist the powerless, those who are powerless will remain helpless and ignored. Some countries help the poor and powerless more than other countries; some help them less. But no country ignores them completely, nor is any country completely egalitarian. The concept of distributive justice has been a subject of ideological debate because it means taking from those who have more and giving to those who have less, so that no one will fall below a minimum, whatever that may be.

In the market-minimized/market-maximized continuum, with political values constant, the subject of ongoing debate is the proper pluralism—the proper mix of private and public functions and responsibilities. The liberal-democratic nations represent a dynamic interrelationship of two philoso-phies—market-minimized and market-maximized—resulting in "mixed" pluralistic characteristics. Each nation has a concept of distributive justice, and each is caught in a political process that Reinhold Niebuhr went to the heart of: "Politics will, to the end of history, be an area where conscience and power meet, where the ethical and coercive factors of human life will interpenetrate and work out their tentative and uneasy compromises."[5]

Out of this social matrix has emerged the welfare state, concerned with mitigating if not eliminating problems caused by severance from the labor market and consequent loss of income. Two premises underlying the welfare state are that individuals cannot be blamed for being unemployed if the economic system does not provide them with jobs[6] and that it is a function of government to provide a minimum subsistence for those unable to provide it for themselves.

Although the line separating market-minimized from market-maximized is drawn through the middle of the continuum in the diagram, it was further toward the righthand side, the market-maximized extreme, during the nineteenth century than it is now. As the line moves toward the left, or market-minimized side, there is not necessarily an increase in state ownership of the means of production but rather an increase in the ap-plication of fiscal and monetary controls and related measures short of actual ownership and operation of the engines of production.[7] Belief in progress persists—a belief (quite new in human history) that human beings through social and political institutions can increase and share goods and services to produce a better life for all.

The difference between the two extremes of the continuum depends on the pace and method of change. The right end of the continuum draws on the classical economic and political theory of change through the market and through limited, representative government. Such change may be fast or slow, but it is organic to the system and its pace is natural: it is incremental, not revolutionary. The left end of the continuum draws on the socialistic doctrine of planned economies and government programs for distributive justice and aspires to change with deliberate speed and at a scheduled pace.

It is largely future-oriented and ahistorical, if not antihistorical. The old is inadequate or corrupt or both; the new and unknown future is good.

Finally, societies on the right end of the continuum believe that rational individuals know what they want and will seek it by competition; just rewards go to the ambitious, and the weak are accorded some sort of minimum subsistence. Societies on the left end of the continuum regard individuals as cooperative and altruistic, given a socialistic structure under which government facilitates these characteristics by collective efforts. It would seem, however, that both extremes are essentially utopian. Throughout history there have been tensions between various factions in a society. The liberal-democratic contribution would seem to be one of managing these tensions and conflicts through the political process.

Before the inauguration of the official social insurance programs to offset lack of income caused by unemployment, disability, or old age, there sprang up in the early developing countries, such as the United Kingdom, Germany, France, and the United States, a great many self-help associations of workers (usually skilled tradesmen) called benefit associations and friendly societies. They were voluntary organizations to which members periodically contributed small sums of money to help each other in case of death, unemployment, and sickness. Governments regarded these associations favorably, as evidence of self-reliance and prudence—qualities that kept workers off the tax-supported welfare rolls. Parsimonious public assistance for paupers was not intended for the working, low-income element of the labor force. There was also some form of private charity. Even in the early days of industrialization it appeared that there would be a modest social surplus beyond bare subsistence.

The sharing of this social surplus, however, was and is a highly controversial political issue inherent in the taxing power of the state. The increase in the social surplus enabled the creation of various government-sponsored welfare and health measures, using the ultimate power lodged in the state to raise money through property taxes, personal and corporate income taxes, excise taxes, taxes on goods and services, and payroll taxes. There was a concurrent increase in the private sector in various types of life insurance, burial insurance, disability insurance, and insurance to meet the costs of personal health services. In the liberal-democratic political process, methods of financing, levels of benefits, and specifications of rights to benefits have been fiercely negotiated and bargained for.

Depending on the position in the continuum that the parties at interest occupied while various welfare and health measures and their financing were debated, what emerged was a mix of means tests, specified benefits for specified rights, payroll deductions, and personal income tax. The clear trend has been toward the use of a means test for public assistance as a residue of an increasingly expanding concept of social insurance, and away from the use instead of a character test. As for a character test, as early as 1909 Winston Churchill attacked the notion that one member of the Royal Commission on the Poor had suggested—that workers not be given unemployment benefits if they were discharged for drunkenness. Churchill's pithy retort was, "I do not like mixing up moralities and mathematics."[8]

An income maintenance program is easy to administer, however, in comparison with health insurance. There are two distinctly different ways of handling the untoward costs of personal health services. Protection can take the form of an indemnity from an insurance company or from the state, in which case the beneficiaries become buyers of services. Or the state can provide health services with little or no charge at the time of services, in which case the beneficiaries receive services but are not buyers. The first is called insurance, and the other is called a health service.

The more one agrees with the position toward the right end of the continuum, the more likely one is to favor private insurance that covers all sorts of contingencies, including unexpected costs of personal health services. As one approaches the position toward the left end of the continuum, one eventually subscribes to a health service completely owned, financed, and salaried by the state and paid for out of general revenue.

On the right-hand side of the continuum, one is likely to believe in cash indemnity for health services and financial controls on patients. This view regards providers of services as essentially autonomous sellers of services; patients, as it were, hire a physician to manage their service needs. On the left-hand side of the continuum, with the highly structured and completely government-owned health service, there would be no charge to the patient at the time of service. Charges to the patient at that time, no matter how small they were, would be regarded as an undesirable barrier to access to services for prevention, early diagnosis, and treatment. At the right-hand extreme, patients are assumed to know their self-interest well enough not to be inhibited by charges at the time of service.

The debate over the allocation of the social surplus for health purposes is growing more intense as health services press on the gross national product, government priorities, and employer contributions—the last of which result in higher prices for products. The debate probes the issues of rational use of technology, equitable access to services, the management of care, the containment of costs, effective forms of rationing, and the efficient delivery of medical services. The debate goes on in all liberal democracies, and it will yield different results across the market-minimized/market-maximized continuum.

In the chapters that follow, seven liberal democracies and their health care delivery systems will be considered in the context of the continuum.

Countries formulate health policy within the segments of the continuum in which they find themselves. Each country has a limited range of political options. Each segment of the continuum in which countries function is taken as a given that shifts slowly over time.

Notes

1. Gerard DeGré, "Freedom and Social Structure," *American Sociological Review* 11 (October 1946): 529–36.
2. Colin Clark, *The Conditions of Economic Progress*, 2d ed. (London: Macmillan, 1951). See also Carlo M. Cipolla, ed., *The Fontana Economic History of Europe* (Glasgow: Fontana Books, 1976); Andrew Boltho, ed., *The European Economy* (New York: Oxford University Press, 1982).
3. Robert A. Dahl and Charles E. Lindblom, *Politics, Economics, and Welfare* (New York: Harper & Row, 1953), p. 511.
4. DeGré, "Freedom and Social Structure," pp. 529–36.
5. Reinhold Niebuhr, *Moral Man and Immoral Society: A Study in Ethics and Politics* (New York: Scribners, 1983), p. 3.
6. This is a very brief description of extremely complicated social, economic, and political transformations. The literature is vast; representative selected titles are: Walter Lippman, *The Good Society: An Inquiry into the Principles of a Good Society* (New York: Little, Brown & Co., 1937); Karl Polanyi, *The Great Transformation* (New York: Farrar and Rinehart, 1944); Joseph H. Schumpeter, *Capitalism, Socialism, and Democracy* (New York: Harper Torch Books, 1962); Max Weber, *The Protestant Ethic and the Spirit of Capitalism*, trans. A. M. Henderson and Talcott Parsons (Glencoe, IL: Free Press, 1964); Harold L. Wilensky and Charles N. Lebeaux, *Industrial Society and Social Welfare* (New York: Russell Sage Foundation, 1958); and Peter L. Berger, *The Capitalist Revolution: Fifty Propositions about Prosperity, Equality and Liberty* (New York: Basic Books, 1986).
7. Andrew Shonfield, *Modern Capitalism: The Changing Balance of Public and Private Power* (London: Oxford University Press, 1969); Dahl and Lindbloom, *Politics, Economics, and Welfare*, p. 10.
8. Bentley B. Gilbert, *The Evolution of National Health Insurance in Great Britain: The Origins of the Welfare State* (London: Michael Joseph, 1966), p. 232.

Part II

Case Studies in the Continuum

In Part II of this book, I consider one by one and in detail seven states along the market-minimized/market-maximized continuum, starting with the United Kingdom which lies nearer the market-minimized pole than any other country in the liberal-democratic orbit. I discuss Sweden, Canada, West Germany, France, and Australia, moving along the continuum to the United States, the liberal democracy nearest the market-maximized pole.

All of the economies in the continuum are mixed as to the interrelationship of the private and public sectors, but the proportions of the mixture vary. The degree to which a state centralizes financing and planning and the relative size of its public sector determine its position in the continuum, as does the extent to which it intervenes in the operation of the economy itself.

The conceptualization and conduct of empirical studies of the mix of private and public functions and responsibilities is a complicated undertaking, even for economists, not to mention those like me with a general social science training largely in sociology. I will not engage in private- and public-sector economic analysis—I will limit myself to discussion of the private-public mix of the health services sector of the economy—but I will suggest that my conceptualization appears reasonable as far as it goes and is sufficient for my purpose in this book.

In the case studies I pay little attention to the standard and traditional public health services of environmental sanitation and communicable disease control because these services have been publicly financed and administered since shortly after the middle of the nineteenth century. Environmental sanitation and communicable disease control were rightly assumed to be beyond the control of individual households. Personal health services, however, were regarded as a personal problem for those who were not destitute; individuals were expected to arrange their personal health services for themselves. Over time, personal health services have increasingly been viewed as a collective responsibility, but each country differs in the extent to which it uses government to assume the responsibility.

I selected the United Kingdom, Sweden, Canada, West Germany, France, Australia, and the United States for extensive presentation in this book because of their relative positions in the market-minimized/market-maximized continuum and because of the relative abundance of information and data about them. I have read their histories, and I have assembled current data on the various countries in large part through frequent visits— which facilitate firsthand contacts and the collection of materials—particularly in the cases of Canada, the United Kingdom, Sweden, and the United States. For West Germany, France, and Australia, I depended largely on official documents, other publications, and correspondence.

In addition Frank Place, a graduate student in economics, did a thorough job of searching out all the existing data on facilities, personnel, expenditures, utilization, and components of service to the extent these data were available, retrospectively and currently (up to 1982 in some instances). The major sources were the annual volumes of the United Nations Demograhic Yearbook, the reports of the Organization for Economic Cooperation and Development, and official publications of the countries themselves.

More systematic and organized sources are listed here. Marshall W. Raffel, editor of *Comparative Systems: Descriptive Analyses of Fourteen National Health Systems* (University Park, PA: Pennsylvania State University Press, 1984), had a person in each of 14 countries prepare a description of the organization and funding sources of the country's health services delivery system, number of beds, personnel, and expenditures, according to a common format. It was an ambitious, international, collaborative undertaking quite successfully carried out. It was not, however, a macro synthesis of cross-national experiences with the organization and financing of health services delivery systems. The book gives the reader a sense of the descriptive differences of systems, from highly developed to developing, and a feeling for the nature and volume of the statistical data available.

Another source is Alan Maynard's descriptive and comparative work, *Health Care in the European Community* (Pittsburgh: University of Pittsburgh Press, 1975). A third is the path-breaking attempt to make sense out of the different expenditure patterns of the developed countries in Europe and of the United States, Canada, and Australia by Robert J. Maxwell—*Health and Wealth: An International Study of Health-Care Spending* (Lexington, MA: Lexington Books, 1981). This is a cross-national study of a given time period, 1974–75, and thus misses the analytic advantage of differentiated trends among countries. The cross-sectional comparisons at a given time were a heroic project, however, and should be given due credit.

A much less statistical survey over years of travel, consultation with governments, and judicious impressions is provided for developing and developed countries by Milton I. Roemer, *Health Care Systems in World Perspective* (Ann Arbor, MI: Health Administration Press, 1976).

Finally, there is my book in which I attempted to combine historical, statistical, and current cross-national comparisons of three countries representing a range of loosely structured to highly structured systems and showing the historical reasons for their systems' structure. Odin W. Anderson, *Health Care: Can There be Equity? The United States, Sweden and England* (New York: John Wiley & Sons, 1972) is out of date for the period since 1970, but it is still relevant.

For particular countries the following have published exceedingly good statistical data in systematic format historically and currently: for Great Britain, Office of Health Economics, *Compendium of Health Statistics*, 5th ed. (London: The Office, 1984); for France, Andrée Mizrahi, Arié Mizrahi, and Simone Sandier, *Medical Care, Morbidity and Costs: Graphic Presentations of Health Statistics* (Oxford: Pergamon Press, 1983); and for Canada, Department of Health and Welfare, *National Health Expenditures in Canada, 1970–1982* (Ottawa: The Department, n.d.). For the United States there are the annual publications of *Health United States* by the U.S. Department of Health and Human Services, and the annual and retrospective (to 1919) summaries of national expenditures in the *Health Care Financing Review* of the Health Care Financing Administration. Extremely valuable (and fortunately available before the completion of this book) is the Organization for Economic Cooperation and Development's *Measuring Health Care, 1960–1983: Expenditures, Costs and Performance*, Social Policy Studies No. 2 (Paris: The Organization, 1985) and *Financing and Delivering Health Care: A Comparative Analysis of OECD Countries*, Social Policy Studies No. 4 (Paris: The Organization, 1987). Ray H. Elling's global study of system differences, *Cross-National Study of Health Systems: Political Economics and Health Care* (New Brunswick, NJ: Transaction Books, 1980), should also be mentioned. Elling's objective was to show the influence of the major political economic systems—democratic, capitalist, and socialist-communist—on the organizational financing of health services with particular reference to equity. I limit myself in the present work to the liberal-democratic range.

Chapter 3

The United Kingdom

Before 1900

The British National Health Service represents the market-minimized extreme in the liberal-democratic continuum, but it had a long development. The industrial revolution, given further stimulus by the dismantling of the mercantile state stemming from the Reform Act of 1832, allowed the burgeoning middle, entrepreneurial, and professional classes to be elected to Parliament. The laissez faire concept of limited government became dominant. During the rest of the nineteenth century, the limited government, laissez faire concept, so far as health and welfare were concerned, was expressed in the official separation of the poor from the rest of society through restrictive means tests for subsistence, workhouses where even families were separated, and means tests for physicians' services and hospital care. Physician care was usually provided by comparatively low-paid physicians employed by the local boards of guardians, those boards comprising leading citizens steeped in the tradition of benevolent paternalism and noblesse oblige. As more scientifically based medicine emerged during the last quarter of the nineteenth century, the old and venerable hospitals subsidized by the new rich and by the still rich, landed aristocracy were turned into more modern facilities fit for surgical operations and medical patients. These voluntary hospitals were established to care for the working poor. The care of paupers—the "undeserving" poor, the residue of human misery—was subsidized from tax revenue in municipal hospitals for the poor. To serve the upper middle class and the rich, the voluntary hospitals set aside a portion of the beds for private patients. In addition, there also emerged what the British then called nursing homes, actually small private hospitals for the upper middle classes and the rich.[1]

In the nineteenth century, physicians were mainly in private practice, presumably living in genteel poverty at best, except for an emerging elite of surgical and medical specialists who gained admission privileges to the prestigious voluntary hospitals and the right to have private patients. In turn, these physicians provided free care to the deserving poor and admitted their private patients to the private accommodations of the voluntary hospitals from their private offices on Harley or Wimpole streets in London and equiv-alent streets in other cities. Later in the century, the fairly numerous general practitioners also had part-time appointments as physicians for the "friendly" and "benefit" societies established by skilled workers, with possi-bly some help from employers as well. This became known as panel prac-tice. Physicians were paid a certain amount per head for a year or some other period. Accordingly, a fairly distinct three-class health services system developed, consisting of (1) paupers, (2) the working class, and (3) the upper classes, each with a quite distinct hierarchy of facilities and physicians. The main distinction among types of physicians was that of in-hospital specialists versus out-of-hospital practitioners. The latter, in order to place their patients in the voluntary hospitals, had to refer them to the specialists.

1900–1946

A Conservative government established a Royal Commission on the Poor Laws in 1906 to look into the condition of the poor, whose numbers were not decreasing despite a relatively prosperous, growth economy. Al-though the commission's emphasis was on material subsistence and income, it paid some attention to the health services. The commission was split between those who favored a public system of personal health services for persons with low income and those who favored a social insurance ap-proach. The Conservatives, including the Fabian Socialists, Beatrice and Sidney Webb, wanted a public health service financed by general revenue. The Liberals preferred financing by insurance and payroll deduction, build-ing on the existing Friendly and Benefit Societies and the insurance industry. The Conservatives had their roots in the landed aristocracy's noblesse oblige of caring for their charges, while the Liberals had theirs in the laissez faire theories of Adam Smith, the market, and the idea of self-help which the Friendly and Benefit Societies embodied. The Liberal party came into power in 1909. Labor, although increasingly organized, did not yet have its own party.

The working class did, however, have a swing vote and a great deal of interest in the maintenance and strengthening of their Friendly Societies. An influential segment of the working class consisted of the skilled workers who were becoming integrated into the mainstream of the production and distribution system. The relatively unskilled and lower paid one-third of the working class was still close to pauper status and very vulnerable. Possibly, the entire working class made up 80 percent of the population, the remainder being paupers, the middle class, and the aristocracy. To remain in power the Liberal party appealed to the working class by instituting pension schemes and health insurance. The comment of the time echoed the conservative Bismarck in Germany in 1883: the Liberal party "spiked the Socialists' guns." The health insurance law passed in 1911 was a rather limited one, however, directed to general practitioners' services for workers below a certain income, and it even excluded dependents. Dependents were to rely on the generosity of the general practitioners in private practice, the voluntary hospitals, and as a last resort the public municipal hospitals and the local boards of guardians. Great Britain was then on the road to social insurance based on the Continental pattern, a natural spin-off of capitalism, laissez faire, and liberal democracy.

In the early 1920s, however, the Liberal party went out of power, and thereafter, Great Britain became mainly a two-party political system of Labour and Conservatives, with profound consequences for the shape of the British health services and their financing when the current National Health Service was put into place in 1946 after the end of World War II.

From the early 1920s through World War II, the British health services were highly pluralistic, even more so than the contemporary and current patterns in the United States. Welfare health services for the statutory poor continued through the public hospitals and the Poor Law physicians; general practitioners' services for the working classes were covered by the National Health Insurance Act of 1911. Hospital insurance for the working class through contributory schemes was growing, as were similar schemes for the middle classes. The whole structure rested on a deteriorating hospital physical plant. Private philanthropy for capital subsidies were no longer adequate. The middle classes, despite voluntary health insurance, were beginning to feel the effect of high-cost medical episodes even then, and naturally, public services or charity were not acceptable options.

By 1945, at the end of World War II, which had brought total mobilization of people and resources, Great Britain was in many ways a transformed country. The euphoria of solidarity found expression in the concept of the National Health Service and resulted in the coalescence of the British Conservative tradition of noblesse oblige and the Socialist objectives of solidarity and equality. This is not to say that the middle road of insurance was not discussed. The Conservative and the Labour (Socialist) views won out, however, and the seeming anomaly of a national health service in a country which originated both the industrial revolution and the concept of a limited government was established. The idea of a national health service transcended the laissez faire, limited government philosophy which Great Britain generally continues to have for the economy.

The political debate that took place during World War II on the shape of the welfare state to come after the war was mainly centered on health services. The National Health Service is regarded as the keystone of the British welfare state. With the coalescence of the two traditions, the insurance of risk, payroll deduction, and selected services rather than comprehensive services did not remain in the debate arena very long. By 1945 four principles were agreed on as the bedrock of the structure and funding of the public services including the traditional public health programs. Health services were to be: (1) universal, (2) comprehensive, (3) free to the user, and (4) financed by general revenue from the national treasury. Universality was to be absolute; no one was to be left out or divided into special categories. Comprehensive services meant just that: all services professionally regarded as such would be included. There would be no charge to the patient at the time of use of services. Last and most telling, the National Health Service would be financed from the national treasury from general revenue, which in large part meant the progressive personal income tax. This principle would facilitate the sharing of the financial burden among the income classes, and the centralization of criteria and financing would facilitate the gradual equalization of access to services and the distribution of the supply of facilities and personnel. It was (and is) a dazzling concept in the post–World War II emergence of the liberal-democratic concept of the welfare state.

The political battles between the providers, chiefly the physicians, and the Labour government under which the National Health Service Act was enacted in 1946, were intense. The act in principle always had bipartisan support. There were two fronts: the consultants in the hospitals with private practices versus the general practitioners, a traditional division which had evolved over the generations. The consultants feared the loss of their private practice prerogatives and the threat of a salaried service that implied a civil service status. The general practitioners feared they would be herded into health centers and salaried, thus losing their traditional combination of panel practice, capitation, and fee-for-service for private patients. The Labour Minister of Health, Aneurin Bevan, was a crafty negotiator with a keen sense of compromise, a pragmatic socialist as it were. Sensing the deep hostility of the consultants and their power and prestige in the British Establishment (their specialty societies had names preceded by the word Royal), Bevan won the consultants over by offering high salaries ("lined their teeth with gold"), permanent tenure, and the right to part-time hospital appointments and private patients. Bevan feared that many high grade consultants would either not sign up, emigrate, or go mainly into private practice, thus diluting the quality of service. The general practitioners were freed of the immediate threat of health centers and of the salary method of payment by the continuation of panel practice and the capitation method of payment, to which virtually all the general practitioners had become accustomed. They could also have private, fee-paying patients. The general public was accorded the right to free choice among the general practitioners, who would serve as entry points to the system.

The voluntary hospitals were no particular political problem, although they were rather badly off after the war because of their financial inability to maintain the physical plants, not to mention building new hospitals. The public hospitals, owned by the cities, were likewise no political problem. So, in one fell swoop the hospitals were "nationalized"—too strong a word in the British political context, because the hospitals were quite glad to be relieved of the burden beyond their fiscal management and control. Thus, they came under the full ownership and control of the central government, and the physicians became contracting agents with the government outside of the civil service system. The dentists became contracting agents on a fee-for-service basis. All other providers—pharmacists, optometrists, vendors of hearing aids, prosthetic devices, and so on—were contractors with the National Health Service.

The structure that was created to implement the four principles described above flowed quite naturally from them. The organizational structure which was set up in 1946 and which went into operation in 1948 can be described simply and briefly, although this belies the complexity of the many interests and their relationships within it. From 1948 to 1974 the National Health Service had three parallel divisions reporting to the Minister of Health, who is a member of the House of Commons and the party in power and hence a member of the cabinet. Naturally, the Treasury wields tremendous power in the setting of national priorities and allocation of funds to the numerous enterprises assigned to modern governments.

The first of the three parallel divisions consisted of the hospitals and included the specialists in a salaried hierarchy by means of a consultant for each specialty which was allotted a number of beds under its control. The hospitals were divided into 14 regions for England and Wales, with Northern Ireland and Scotland separate regions with the same internal structure. Each region was to have a teaching hospital. The teaching hospitals were not a part of the regional hospital governing body but reported as a group directly to the Minister of Health. This arrangement was a concession to the teaching hospitals and their prestigious consultants, who feared being smelted into the less specialized hospitals, thus reducing their political clout for funds. The concept of the hospital as a separate administrative and fiscal entity through the boards was, of course, also a concession to the power of the consultants, and for that matter, to the high regard of the public as well. These are the visible symbols of healing. Each hospital region had a governing body called the regional hospital board. The boards were appointed through consultations with the Minister and the regional parties of interest representing the usual variety of constituencies and prominent citizens. They served without pay and carried enormous responsibilities in that they reviewed and approved the distribution, delivery, and costs of hospital-based services, the most expensive and technical component of the system. These boards are a carry-over from the voluntary hospital boards, signifying continuation of the British tradition of voluntary boards for public purposes, an amalgam of private-public constituencies quite peculiar to Great Britain but adopted among the liberal-democratic countries in the United States and the Commonwealth countries.

Under the regional hospital boards there were 400 hospital management committees concerned with the daily operation of hospitals. Again, the Management Committees were made up of unpaid members appointed in consultation with the local interest groups and the regional hospital board. Their administrative staffs worked rather intensively with the hospitals and even departments within hospitals. It then follows that each hospital had little autonomy with respect to facilities and equipment, in contrast to the great autonomy the voluntary hospitals had had before the National Health Service.

The second administratively and fiscally parallel division was responsible for general practitioner, dental, pharmaceutical, optical, and prosthetic services and products. Local executive councils contracted for and administered these ambulatory services. The councils—138 of them in England and Wales—had an appointed, unpaid, and voluntary membership. It should be noted that the regional and local executive boundaries were not coterminous. This parallel division of the general practitioners was a concession to their desire to have a direct line to the Minister and the Treasury so as not to be smothered, in their view, by the resource-gobbling power of the consultants.

Finally, the third parallel division in the National Health Service was composed of the 148 local health authorities. These were the original local public health agencies owned and funded by the local governments through local tax rates. They retained control over the traditional public health functions of environmental sanitation, communicable disease control, and maternal and child health. In Great Britain the public health officers had run the public city hospitals but were relieved of this responsibility in the new structure. The creation of the local health authorities was again a concession to the old and established public health departments. The public health officers were shifted in the new structure from wholly local funding and responsibility to partial funding and control, with the budget divided between the local and national levels. In the new structure, the old and characteristic separations between the hospital, the general practitioner, and the public health officer were institutionalized even more through law. Proponents of an integrated acute care–preventive care structure had to wait until 1974 to break down the arbitrary divisions between them in the organizational structure of 1946.

John Pater, a senior civil servant engaged in the process, observed the creation of the National Health Service. His observations reveal the incremental political styles in liberal-democratic political systems.

> However imperfect the result, the makers of NHS did the best that was possible in the context of the 1940s. They worked out a pattern and an organization of services which appeared likely to be efficient and, in all subsequent exchanges, they sought to approximate as nearly as possible to the original concepts [the four principles]. The other parties involved, notably the medical profession, had the weight and political strength to compel some modifications, but the main objectives remained secure. The keynote of the whole process might be described as evolutionary pragmatism—pragmatism because the ideal was continually being adapted to practicalities, and evolutionary because the whole control and structure were rooted in the experience of the past and the circumstances of the period. There were voices, again notably medical, calling for lesser and more gradual change—for example, as a first step the extension of NHI [National Health Insurance of 1911], and the regionalization of hospital services—but the makers of the NHS saw that if the opportunity of war-time flexibility were not seized to introduce a comprehensive service, the goal might be missed for many years.[2]

There was an overriding consensus for the National Health Service concept that could not, politically, be successfully resisted. If there had been a Liberal party, as in 1911 when that party succeeded in enacting the National Health Insurance Act based on actuarial insurance principles, it is not likely that a health service of the type embodied in the National Health Service would have been conceived. The Conservatives and the Labour Socialists drew on the roots of their respective traditions and values as far as the health services were concerned. Thus the break with the past as embodied in the new National Health Service structure was not as radical as it first appeared. The National Health Service was still a product of political incrementalism, although it came about quite suddenly.

1946–1974

On July 5, 1948 the National Health Service went into effect. It is said that a patient in a hospital bed on July 4 waking up in the same bed on July 5 was not aware of the change of ownership, sources of revenue, and the new status of the attending consultant. Physicians, both consultants and general practitioners, were certainly aware. And by the end of the fiscal year the

Treasury and the government found that the costs of health services had been grossly underestimated. Deficit financing reached a politically significant magnitude. It had been naively assumed that a health service would in a short time reduce the reservoir of illness by clearing up unmet needs and thus result in lower expenditures. A later Minister of Health, Enoch Powell, remarked that it was a "miscalculation of sublime proportions."

As observed by Pater, what became known as the tripartite structure of the National Health Service was a political compromise among professional groups. In short order, there was dissatisfaction with the divided structure, which was partially blamed for the deficits. The structure inhibited central control over all components of service within regions. Each of the tripartite divisions had its own budget. If all of the components of the service could be under one authority, region by region, the regional boards, it was thought, could then integrate all service components into one budget through fiscal control and achieve a "balanced" range and proportion of services. The tripartite structure met sporadic criticism until the late 1960s and early 1970s. In the meantime, nevertheless, the National Health Service was an enormous public success and, therefore, a political success. The public was freed from the fear of costly illnesses; the funding came from general revenue, which gave the illusion (except to the Treasury) that the service was free; and there was an improvement in the distribution of consultants throughout the country—many new positions were created in outlying hospitals. There was also some improvement in the distribution of general practitioners. The National Health Service divided the country into underserved, adequately served, and overserved areas for general practitioners. They were no longer free to set up their practices anywhere they wished but were induced to go to areas that were deficient.

Although expenditures for the British health services as measured by gross national product have been significantly lower than those for other industrial countries, it is pertinent to note that the British increase in expenditures has been roughly of the same magnitude as the increase in other countries, presumably starting from a lower base. For one thing, Britain did relatively little to replace or expand its hospital stock. Hence, unlike France, West Germany, the United States, and Sweden, Britain has had a lower capital investment. It has, however, done a remarkable job of making do and fixing up. The hospital bed stock, although reduced, has been quite constant and in quite the same ratio to population as other industrialized countries. A 20-year plan for hospital improvement was officially proposed in the early 1960s, but adequate funding was not supplied.

After 1950 there was concern with the rapidly rising expenditures. In addition, the physicians and dentists began to press for higher salaries, capitation, and fees. In 1956, eight years after the National Health Service was established, and therefore with eight years of financial data and experience, the government set up a committee of inquiry. The evaluation of expenditure trends was made by a Ph.D. student, Brian Abel-Smith of Cambridge University, working with Professor Richard Titmuss of the London School of Economics.[3] Contrary to expectation, the study showed that from 1949 to 1955 the National Health Service had actually decreased its proportion of the gross national product.

The tripartite structure continued to gnaw at the structural propensities of the British political style of organization and administration. If services could be integrated regionally, overlap could be eliminated and overall efficiency could be improved, thus enabling a lower cost (in a service which was the cheapest among all industrialized countries). Regional integration would also weaken the relative influence of the hospital sector and the consultants in favor of out-of-hospital services, long-term care, and home care services. Gradually the political parties, which were quite in agreement on the value of reorganization, coalesced sufficiently to start formulating a plan for reorganization. It should be noted that the principles underlying the concept of the National Health Service—that is it should be universal, comprehensive, free to the user at the time of service, and funded by general revenue—were not in question, nor were the methods of paying physicians. The problem was management, getting more for the money. In 1948, it was the physicians who felt the greatest organizational change. In 1974, when the reorganization took place, it was the administrators who experienced the greatest change.

1974–1982

The reorganized National Health Service which went into operation on April 1, 1974 is a product of the organizational theory of management by consensus.[4] England and Wales were organized into 14 regional health authorities, 90 area health authorities, and 206 district management teams. The regional health authority had total responsibility for the overall planning and allocation of funds in the region, the integration of the entire spectrum of services. The area health authority was the statutory supervisory level for the district, the front-line delivery point for all services except the distribution of blood and emergency ambulance services, which were the responsibility of the regional health authority.

Starting at the bottom, at the district level, there were an administrator, a treasurer, a nursing officer, a medical officer (community physician), and two clinicians—a generalist and a specialist. These functionaries were closest to the people, patients, facilities, and health personnel and were to be the antennae for feeling out local health problems more or less peculiar to each district. The next level, the area health authority, had similar positions, and the staff were to supervise the operation of the district management team. The top level, the regional health authority, also had more or less similar positions, but with the overall planning and fiscal allocation responsibility. The regional health authorities reported to the Secretary of State and the Minister of State (Health), Department of Health and Social Services, who in turn, reported to Parliament and the Treasury.

The staff at each level appointed a chairman—usually the administrator—to officiate at meetings. Policy and operating decisions were made after the staff had discussed the issues and arrived at a consensus (apparently not even voting). Decisions were transmitted to the area health authority, where a similar process took place, and then to the regional health authority. Decisions could also proceed from the top down.

Another innovation was the creation of community health councils made up of disease interest groups and other representatives as watchdogs of the National Health Service. They were financed by the regions and had a paid staff with a secretary. There was emphasis on the need to balance "accountability upwards" by "delegation downwards." The management by consensus concept was based on the theory that, for both physicians (the primary resource allocators) and managers (the custodians of the resources) decisions had to be made mainly on professional and best judgments, in a context that was at once professional and political, and with paucity of valid indicators of the quantity, not to mention the quality, of performance.

The emphasis on consensus showed a recognition that the health services enterprise was essentially a profound negotiating and bargaining process among the parties at interest, resulting in a particular equilibrium of funding, supply of services, utilization, and convenience of access. Deliberately, it seems, no one was to be in charge; no one position was to be held responsible. The Parliament and Treasury held the purse strings and set the national budget within which the actors in the system had to figure out how to spend the money available while meeting the four basic principles. The reorganization worked in that the public continued to regard the National Health Service as fair, free, and universal. From a managerial standpoint it can be said that the 1974 reorganization worked because of the British capacity for joint consultations in endless meetings and for avoidance of confrontations, a most civil civic culture.

But expenditures still continued to increase at an alarming rate in the view of the Treasury and politicians. Management by consensus avoided the pinpointing of management responsibility, and there were critics who felt there were too many layers of authority. The area health authorities were probably unnecessary, and the districts felt so as well. The National Health Service was now being overmanaged! It was in for another round of reorganization—a traumatic experience for the managerial cadre but not for patients and physicians as long as the entry points to the system remained open and supply was more or less constant.

The concern with overmanagement and rising costs eventually resulted in the first Royal Commission on the National Health Service, authorized in 1976 to review the entire health service operation with a very open agenda. Another concern pervading the operation of the service was the increasing restiveness of the hospital-based physicians, particularly the junior staff who complained that being underpaid and overworked resulted in poor quality. They carried out work-to-rule actions, that is, they followed rules to the letter, which led to slowdowns. Nurses and other personnel were also engaging in "industrial actions," as the British call union-style work disruptions. The National Health Service was being dragged into the industrial model of labor negotiations, a far cry from the dedicated service- and charity-oriented tradition of noblesse oblige and the paternalism of the past. Health services personnel, including physicians and nurses, now had the capacity and apparently the will to stop the functioning of health care services on a national scale except for a skeleton staff to take care of dire emergencies. The issue of the role of private medical practice and private health insurance was also being raised whenever the Labour government was in power, an issue always under the surface. Although private expenditure was relatively small, less than 1 percent of total expenditures at the time, it raised the principle of equity. A Hospital Act of 1976 mandated a gradual elimination of private beds in NHS hospitals, but the election of a Conservative government in 1979 stopped the process.

The Royal Commission on the National Health Service in 1976 was made up of the usual representatives of interest groups, but with only one representative of the medical profession, who was a general practitioner, not a consultant. It also had an academic economist who was active in the economics of health. The director was a chancellor of one of the British universities. A first class technical staff was assembled to listen to testimony and conduct and authorize pertinent studies.

The commission, in addition to its own report, commissioned other excellent reports on decision making in the contemporary organizational structure, on the financial structure, on accounting and controls, and a survey of public attitudes toward the service, particularly toward the hospital sector, and of smaller studies.[5] The final recommendations of the commission ranged from those for specific details to major policy. An example of detail was the recommendation that since many patients complained about being awakened at five o'clock in the morning to fit into the hospital routine, they should be awakened later; an example of major policy was the recommendation to abolish the area health authorities.

The private sector was examined quite thoroughly but not encouraged, since encouragement could be seen as eroding the original objective of the service. The commission did not question the substance of the service, but it did point out that improvements could be made here and there. An increase in funding was regarded as essential to maintaining the service's integrity. The commission could hardly recommend a narrowing of benefits or insurance: the service was too embedded in the very fabric of British society for such changes. The study on the management of financial resources contains this observation: "The NHS continues to be—whatever its problems and worries of the moment—an invaluable source of welfare and peace of mind for the inhabitants of Britain."[6]

The royal commission reported in 1979. The next major step was the elimination of the area health authority tier in 1982 under a Conservative government and elimination of the management-by-consensus concept. Individual accountability for management was inaugurated. The consensus concept was not congenial to a business and profit-making structure, and it was felt business management concepts could be applied to a publicly funded enterprise.

In 1976, the same year the royal commission was established, a working party appointed by the Department of Health and Social Security (DHSS) reported after several years of study and deliberation on how resources for health services could and should be shared.[7] The 14 regions in England and Wales were classified by the age and composition of the population, the number of hospital beds, and the rates of mortality, disability, and acute illness. A formula was devised relating need to resources through epidemiological information. There had been a wide variation in hospital beds, by as much as 100 percent, a legacy of the distribution of beds since 1948. The long-range plan was to reduce variations between regions by fiscal controls. Somewhat belatedly it seems, considering the planning possibilities in the National Health Service structure, the DHSS began to consider equality of distribution of facilities in addition to equality of access by eliminating the economic barriers. The tripartite structure, as mentioned, had made planning difficult; the new 1974 structure would facilitate planning among and within regions and would, presumably, get more for the money by reducing the use of hospitals and increasing the use of out-of-hospital services. Still, we must remember that directed planning, in terms of giving orders, is not congenial to the British political style or to liberal democracies generally. Rather, there is an endless process of consultations and negotiations. With the working party report, the DHSS had at least some guidelines for the regions, backed by the power to close hospitals and fiscal clout. Even here, however, the DHSS had to consider the strength of the feelings of local citizen groups that could operate through the community health councils and veto decisions of the minister. The minister had the power to override the veto, but this could not be a casual decision in the politically charged circumstances.

After the action of the Conservative government in 1982 to eliminate the area health authorities and the consensus management structure, the regional health authorities and the districts remained, as did the types of supervisory and operational personnel on the two levels. The districts continued as the front line of delivery of the full range of services mandated by the National Health Service. The implementation of the concept of direct responsibility in place of consensus management was embodied in the National Health Service Management Inquiry conducted by Roy Griffiths, a businessman, at the request of the Conservative government. He reported in October 1983. His observation was that unlike business operations the health service lacked a clearly defined general management function. He indicated that there was a need to concentrate responsibility in one person at all levels of the organization. In consensus management no one was in charge. Consequently, decision making was far too slow for expeditious administration, and it was extremely difficult to achieve change. The royal commission report had also contained many complaints from personnel of the slowness of decision making. Further, Griffiths held that all unit managers of institutions, of general practitioners' services, and so on, should have a budget for which they were responsible. Thus, there must be delegation of authority all the way down the line. There should be incentives for efficiency and savings to be used at lower levels according to their discretion. Overarching the entire management of the National Health Service should be a management board on the business model, accountable to the DHSS.[8]

There was a critical although sympathetic rejoinder to the Griffiths report from two people from the King Edward's Hospital Fund in London, who represented themselves. In brief, Tom Evans and Robert Maxwell felt the Griffiths recommendations were in the right direction but did not show enough understanding of the nuances and complexities of an enterprise like the National Health Service. The service deals mainly with physicians who need a great deal of discretion in diagnosis and treatment of sick people.[9] Evans and Maxwell wrote that they believed Griffiths and his staff had underestimated the problems of melding the key professional groups—particularly physicians and nurses—into general management, as "[e]ach group has its own tasks, skills, discipline and organization. . . . The current management arrangements (whatever their faults) recognized these differences and sought to cope with them through representatives of professional groups within the management structure."[10] What Evans and Maxwell meant was that professionals cannot be administered through line management, not even in industry.

The National Health Service is implementing the Griffiths concept.

The most recent appraisal of this implementation is a study by Stephen Harrison, in which Harrison concludes that the shift of control from doctors to management has not moved very much so far. In fact, he writes, "Managers neither were nor are supposed to be influential with respect to doctors."[11] It should be noted, however, that management in any context in liberal democratic cultures requires some consensus in order to function.

In the meantime the National Health Service, a tenacious institution, keeps on functioning, in essence according to the four original principles. A debate, whose seriousness is difficult to determine, is taking place on the role of private medicine in relation to the health service; "privatization" is symptomatic of the government's desire to relieve the Treasury and the taxes on the public of some of the cost of health services in the country. Currently, the phenomenon is not peculiar to Great Britain, nor is it particularly new. The issue has a specific significance in Britain, however, because the National Health Service was conceived and designed to make the private sector superfluous by funding sufficient resources to provide adequate care for everyone, even if not at a middle-class level of expectations.

1982–1986

Before the existence of the National Health Service, the private sector was embodied in the private health insurance schemes for both the working class and the middle and upper-middle classes and in patients' direct payments to providers. These schemes were in effect abolished, although not made illegal, by the loss of their markets to the National Health Service. Private insurance schemes later revived in the British United Provident Association, and two smaller associations. They were ingeniously tailored to complement, not supplement, the National Health Service, by selling contracts enabling direct access to and a choice of specialists in the National Health Service hospitals. It will be recalled that specialists or consultants bargained for the privilege of part-time appointments so they could also have time for private patients. This is a form of privatization. Another manifestation of complementarity is the access patients with private health insurance can get to private beds in National Health Service hospitals; the number of private hospitals is also increasing. These two resources together are enough to enable private patients to "jump the queue" for elective surgical operations for which there are long waiting lists. An apt summary of the waiting list situation was made in a policy study: "The private patient pays to avoid waiting, the NHS patient waits to avoid paying."[12] The private insurance schemes do not cover relatively rare, very serious, and expensive surgical procedures, for that would increase the premiums considerably. The National Health Service then becomes, in American terminology a "major medical" backup. Patients with serious and life-threatening conditions are admitted to hospitals quickly. The British people may not opt out of the National Health Service by evading taxes for the service; hence, they can move in and out of the private plans and the NHS as is convenient. As of 1988, about 10 percent of the population was enrolled in private insurance schemes. The members were upper level personnel in business, industry, and the civil service. To a large degree the insurance is one of the "perks" for employees paid by employers. In the late 1970s, the electric workers union and the country's police forces became members, much to the consternation of the more left-wing unions in the Labour party.[13]

Another evidence of privatization is the general practitioner deputizing services operating under various names. In the National Health Service, general practitioners are under contract to be accessible to patients 24 hours a day, seven days a week in one form or another. General practitioners have found this requirement increasingly onerous, especially when compared with the requests for their services before the formation of the National Health Service. Many general practitioners have small partnerships and group practices by which they can share calls on nights and weekends, or solo practitioners can make such arrangements with each other, although there may not be enough of such cooperative arrangements. As far back as the 1950s, general practitioners began contracting with services for backup help on nights, weekends, or other days. The deputizing services have 24-hour-a-day telephone operators who tell callers requesting home visits that their general practitioners are not available but that another physician under contract with the deputizing service for home calls can be sent out instead. The physicians who contract with the deputizing services are willing to be on call for certain hours of the week and to be paid on a per session basis. They are generally hospital-based, at a lower level than consultants, or they may be medically qualified researchers who want to earn extra money. The deputizing service provides an automobile and a standard doctor's bag. The general practitioners contract directly with the deputizing service, and the National Health Service is not involved at all. The general practitioners who use such a service may deduct the cost from their business expenses.

The deputizing service is a symptom of the inability of the National Health Service to be sufficiently responsive to public demand for "trivial" needs. The long-time solution of the service was to have been the creation of general practice health centers to facilitate standby services, but these have been slow in coming because of the costs of the necessary capital. Given the discomfiture of the National Health Service with the deputizing services— the service's fear of losing control over standards, for example—it is surprising how little is known about how they operate. Even their numbers are not known with precision. They exist in all cities, and it is estimated that 40 percent of the general practitioners contract with deputizing services, the proportion being much higher in the cities.

Since the Conservative government took over in 1979, privatization has reached a higher level of intensity. The government is actually encouraging more people to buy private insurance, giving them incentives, such as tax deduction, to do so, and thus relieving the drain on the Treasury. Prior to 1979, the private sector was simply tolerated as a necessary compromise in a pluralistic liberal democracy. It provided a safety valve for the small minority who wanted an alternative, but it posed hardly any threat to the basic structure and operation of the National Health Service. More recently the Labour party and other egalitarian-oriented elements have feared that a growth in private health insurance, although relieving the Treasury, would erode the already strained resources of the National Health Service and result in a two-class and unfair system. The solution would be to increase support of the National Health Service so as to make private insurance less attractive.

Another, less portentous, issue is that of hospitals in the service contracting out for catering and laundry services. This is quite a standard practice in U.S. hospitals and raises no privatization issues here, given the absence of a nationalized hospital system in this country. The National Health Service's personnel, however, regard contracting out as a threat to their jobs and an erosion of the integrity and unity of the National Health Service.

The original objective of the National Health Service was to equalize access, later it was to equalize distribution of supply, and then it was to equalize across the population the amount of anxiety caused by ill health and relative access to the health services. Prior to 1979, a Labour government authorized a study to investigate the distribution of mortality and morbidity rates and use of services in relation to variations in need across classes.[14] The study found that, despite over 30 years of the National Health Service, considerable differences in general mortality, infant mortality, and morbidity remained. The recommendations for the correction of these deficiencies were global, formidable, and expensive. They entailed drastic redistribution of services, increased taxes, food distribution programs, increased food allowances, and improved living and working conditions. The report, known as the Black Report after the chairman, came out after the Conservative party returned to power. The Secretary of State reportedly was shocked and dismissed the recommendations with the remark,

> I must make it clear that additional expenditure on the scale which could result from the report's recommendations—the amount involved could be upwards of 2 billion pounds a year—is quite unrealistic in the present or any foreseeable economic circumstances, quite apart from any judgment that may be

formed of the effectiveness of such expenditures in dealing with the problems identified.[15]

The NHS expenditures were then 13 billion pounds a year, thus 2 billion pounds would be a 15 percent increase when the government was trying to hold the increase to less than 3 percent.

I end this chapter by returning to the major concern of the British with the structure of the National Health Service and with managing it well enough to increase its efficiency and maintain its original egalitarian objectives. Such soul searching may go on forever. An astute observer of this phenomenon believes that the 1982 reorganization, although costly in both human and financial terms, was worth the costs for the improvements it made in management, but he cautioned that this should be the end to "NHS reorganization as a managerial tool to be wielded every few years. This is not a plea for stagnation, but rather for different, less brutal methods of change."[16] What those methods should be he does not venture to say. As long as the British can engage in joint consultations, civilized negotiation, and bargaining, they can administer tolerably any organizational structure. There is now some evidence that the application of the guidelines of the resource allocation working party described earlier is showing some convergence between regions through a long-range fiscal policy.

Still the Thatcher government wishes to loosen up the seemingly monolithic bureaucratic character of the National Health Service in two ways: (1) by encouraging private health insurance as an option, and (2) by giving the district the power to contract for services outside of its legal jurisdiction with lower priced hospitals and physicians. This concept is known in government administration as internal competition.[17]

To facilitate political debate, the House of Commons authorized the establishment of a social services committee to gather information and hear testimonies on a wide range of alternatives for "getting more value for the money." The document was released in July 1988 and represents a thorough examination of the National Health Service and of possible changes. Considerable help was provided by the Institute of Health Services Management, a professional association of health service administrators, through the creation of a working party on alternative delivery and funding of health services. The Institute engaged very competent economists, statisticians, and accountants both inside and outside of academia to write analytic papers for rational policy making with full recognition of the political considerations.[18]

On January 31, 1989, while this book was in press, the Thatcher government released a White Paper.[19] The thrust of the White Paper is toward the possibility of creating, from existing National Health Service hospitals, what would be called self-governing hospitals, to provide some competition with National Health Service hospitals. There are proposals to shorten waiting lists, improve facilities and provide more information to the public. The Paper recommends separating the purchase and planning of health services from the provision of health services, and it proposes that general practitioners each be given a budget under their control by which they can buy the cheapest services and goods for their panel patients. In addition, the Paper recommends encouraging private health insurance by providing tax relief to persons, such as the elderly, who buy private health insurance. Further, eight technical Work Papers are in preparation, dealing with the specifics of self-governing hospitals, funding hospital services, general practitioner practice budgets, general practitioner prescribing budgets, capital charging in the hospital and community services, family practitioner services policy and management issues, medical audit, and management of consultants' contracts and distinction awards.

Summary

Politically, the National Health Service has been a smashing public success. Operationally, it has implemented the four mandated principles, but chronic issues of enough money and convenience of access have been severely exacerbated by the problems in the British economy and the growing, inherent costs of health services. Festering in the body politic is the issue of the size of the private sector and its possible threat to the principles and operation of the National Health Service. Access to health care without direct cost is seen as a right, and the ideas of fairness and justice are being jeopardized. It is thus apparent that the United Kingdom has gone through (1) the stage of the development of the health services infrastructure during 1875–1930; (2) the stage of the appearance of third-party payments, starting with national health insurance plus private insurance and culminating in the National Health Service in 1948; and (3) the third stage, that of management and control, which began immediately afterward because costs readily became an issue, and which was intensified in the reorganization of 1974 that abolished the tripartite structure. Reorganization, as such, does not seem as yet to have resolved the cost issue.

The National Health Service is a structural, organizational, and financing method that is an anomaly among western liberal-democracies. This can only be reasonably explained by the persistence of the monarchy and its tradition and the coalescence of noblesse oblige and Christian socialist values in the body politic. Hence, the United Kingdom can easily be classified as being in the extreme market-minimized end of the continuum for health services.

Notes

1. Odin W. Anderson, *Health Care: Can There Be Equity? The United States, Sweden and England* (New York: John Wiley & Sons, 1972). The literature on the National Health Service is voluminous and by and large very rich as is that for the U.S. health services. Being polar types and prominent, these health services attract a great deal of attention. Suffice it for this book to refer up to 1970 or so as a summary of British developments with rather extensive documentation.

   Additional references on the history of the National Health Service since 1970 enrich this book. J. Rogers Hollingsworth and Ellen Jan Hollingsworth, *Voluntary and Public Hospitals in England and Wales* (New Haven, CT: Yale University, Institution for Social and Policy Studies, Program on Non-Profit Organizations, P.S. Working Paper No. 2075, November 1983); J. Rogers Hollingsworth, *The Delivery of Medical Care in England and Wales, 1890–1910* (Madison, WI: University of Wisconsin–Madison, Institute for Research on Poverty, Discussion Paper No. 614-8, 1980); John E. Pater, *The Making of the National Health Service* (London: King Edward's Fund, King's Fund Historical Series No. 1, 1981); Brian Abel-Smith, *The Making of the National Health Service: The First Thirty Years* (London: Her Majesty's Stationery Office, 1978). Another service using a unique macro forces–trends approach is Daniel M. Fox, *Health Policies, Health Politics: The British and American Experience, 1911–1915* (Princeton, NJ: Princeton University Press, 1986).

   The following references are essential to understand the developments since 1970. R. F. L. Logan, J. S. A. Ashley, R. E. Klein, and D. M. Robson, *Dynamics of Medical Care: The Liverpool Study into Use of Hospital Resources* (London: London School of Hygiene and Tropical Medicine, Memoir No. 14, 1972); Roger M. Batistella and Theodore E. Chester, "Reorganization of the National Health Service: Background and Issues in England's Quest for a Comprehensive-Integrated Planning and Delivery System," *Health and Society* 51 (Fall 1973): 489–530; George Godber, *The Health Service: Past, Present and Future* (London: Athlone Press, 1975); Department of Health and Social Security, *Sharing Resources for Health in England. Report of the Resource Allocation Working Party* (London: Her Majesty's Stationery Office, 1976); Department of Health and Social Security, *Priorities for Health and Person Social Services in England: A Consultative Document* (London: Her Majesty's Stationery Office, 1976); J. Enoch Powell, *Medicine and Politics: 1975 and After* (London: Pitman Medical, 1976); Ralph Harris and Arthur Seldon, *Over-Ruled on Welfare: The Increasing Desire for Choice in Education and Medicine and its Frustration by Representative Government* (London: Institute for Economic Affairs, 1979); Rudolph Klein, "Control Participation and the British National Health Service," *Health and Society* 57 (Winter 1979): 70–74; Michael Lee, *Private and National Health Services* (London: Policy Studies Institute, XLIV, No. 578, July 1978); H. S. E. Gravelle and Alan Williams, *Health Service Finance and Resource Management* (London: King's Fund Centre, Project Paper No. RC6, 1980); Kay Richards, *The NHS and Social Services* (London: King's Fund Centre, Project Paper No. RC11, September 1980); Peter A. West, *The Nation's Health and the NHS* (London: King's Fund Centre, Project Paper No. RC14, September 1980); Ruth Levitt, *The People's Voice in the NHS* (London: King Edward's Hospital Fund for London, 1980); Rosemary Davis and Christine Farrell, *Conflict and Consensus* (London: King's Fund Centre, Project Paper No. RC1, March 1980); Rosemary A. Stevens, *The National Health Service in England in 1980: Notes on*

Comparisons and Stresses (Philadelphia: Leonard Davis Institute of Health Economics, University of Pennsylvania, Discussion Paper No. 1, March 30, 1981); Politics of Health Group and Fightback, *Going Private: The Cases Against Private Medicine—A Report* (London: The Group and Fightback, no date but likely 1980); Ann Cartwright and Robert Anderson, *General Practice Revisited: A Second Study of Patients and Their Doctors* (London: Tavistock, 1981); Christopher Ham, *Health Policy in Britain: The Politics and Organization of the National Health Service* (London: Macmillan, 1982); Gordon McLachlan and Alan Maynard, *The Public-Private Mix for Health: The Relevance and Effects of Change* (London: Nuffield Provincial Hospital Trust, 1982); Peter Townsend and Nick Davidson, eds., *Inequities in Health: The Black Report* (London: Penguin, 1982); D. A. Horne, "Contractual Arrangements: NHS Use of the Private Sector," *British Medical Journal* 284 (April 3, 1982): 1060–61; John K. Iglehart, "The British National Health Service Under the Conservatives," *New England Journal of Medicine* 310 (January 5, 1984): 63–67; Iden Wickings, ed., *Effective Unit Management* (London: King Edward's Hospital Fund for London, 1983); Peter Draper and Tony Smart, eds., *Health and the Economy: The NHS Crisis in Perspective*. Proceedings of a conference held on January 6, 1984 at Guy's Hospital Unit for the Study of Health Policy, Department of Community Medicine. (London: Guy's Hospital Medical School, April 1984); Henry J. Aaron and William B. Schwartz, *The Painful Prescription: Rationing Hospital Care* (Washington, DC: Brookings Institution, 1984).

2. John E. Pater, *The Making of the National Health Service* (London: King Edward's Fund, King's Fund Historical Series, No. 1, 1981).

3. Brian Abel-Smith and Richard M. Titmuss, *The Cost of the National Health Service in England and Wales* (Cambridge: Cambridge University Press, National Institute of Economic and Social Research, Occasional Papers 18, 1956).

4. A well-written source by David Taylor on the evolution of the National Health Service structure is found in: Office of Health Economics, *Understanding the NHS in the 1980s* (London: The Office, No. 75, 1984).

5. See Great Britain: Royal Commission on the National Health Service, *The Working of the National Health Service*. Report presented to Parliament (Commd 7615) (London: Her Majesty's Stationery Office, Research Paper No. 1, 1978). Royal Commission on the National Health Service, *Management of the Financial Resources in the National Health Services* (London: Her Majesty's Stationery Office, Research Paper No. 2, 1978). Royal Commission on the National Health Service, *Patients' Attitudes Toward the Hospital Service* (London: Her Majesty's Stationery Office, Research Paper No. 5, 1978).

6. Royal Commission, *Management of the Financial Resources*, p. 4.

7. Department of Health and Social Security, *Sharing Resources for Health in England. Report of the Resource Allocation Working Party* (London: Her Majesty's Stationery Office, 1976).

8. Roy Griffith, "New Management Inquiry." Report to the Secretary of State of Social Services, Department of State and Social Security, October 6, 1983, typewritten.

9. Tom Evans and Robert Maxwell, "Griffiths: Challenge and Response: Evidence to the Select Committee on Social Service," King Edward's Hospital Fund for London, January 1984, typewritten.

10. Ibid., pp. 3, 4.

11. Stephen Harrison, *Managing the National Health Service: Shifting the Frontier?* (London: Chapman and Hall, 1988), p. 51.

12. Michael Lee, *Private and National Health Services* (London: Policy Studies Institute, XLIV, No. 578, July 1978), p. 22.

13. I can hardly do justice to this issue, but a very sophisticated series of papers can be found in Gordon McLachlan and Allan Maynard, *The Public-Private Mix for Health: The Relevance and Effects of Change* (London: Nuffield Provincial Hospital Trust, 1982).

14. Peter Townsend and Nick Davidson, eds., *Inequities in Health: The Black Report* (London: Penguin, 1982); the then government reproduced only a few hundred copies, but Townsend and Davidson edited the report and got it published through Penguin; it sold widely and soon went out of print.

15. Ibid., pp. 16–17.

16. Iden Wickings, ed., *Effective Unit Management* (London: King Edward's Hospital Fund for London, 1983), p. 10.

17. House of Commons, Session of 1987–88, Social Services Committee, Fifth Report, *The Future of the National Health Service* (London: Her Majesty's Stationery Office, House of Commons Paper 613, forthcoming 1988).

18. Institute of Health Services Management, Working Party on Alternative Delivery and Funding of Health Services. There are seven working papers and a final report as follows: Working Paper No. 1. *The Search for a System—Establishing the Criteria*, March 1988; Working Paper No. 2. A. J. Culyer, Cam Donaldson, and Karen Gerard, *Alternatives for Funding Health Services in the U.K.*, March 1988; Working Paper No. 3. A. J. Culyer, Cam Donaldson, and Karen Gerard, *Financial Aspects of Health Services: Drawing on Experience*, March 1988; Working Paper No. 4. A. J. Culyer, and J. E. Brazier, *Alternatives for Organising the Provision of Health Services in the U. K.*, April 1988; Working Paper No. 5. A. J. Culyer, J. E. Brazier, and Owen O'Donnell, *Organising Health Service Provision: Drawing on Experience*, April 1988; Working Paper No. 6. George C. Orros, *The Potential Role of Private Health Insurance*, April 1988; Working Paper No. 7. Malcolm Prowle and Graham Lester, *Capital in the NHS*, May 1988; *Final Report of the Working Party*, June 1988. All the working papers and the report are published by the Institute of Health Services Management, London.

19. *Working for Patients*. Presented to Parliament by the Secretaries of State for Health—Wales, Northern Ireland, and Scotland by command of Her Majesty, January 1989. (London: Her Majesty's Stationery Office, 1989).

Chapter 4

Sweden

Before 1862

Sweden is the largest and most populous of the five countries in the Scandinavian cultural and political orbit (Denmark, Finland, Iceland, Norway, and Sweden). They share a common political heritage of balancing local and central power. Local governments, called here county councils, have always been strong in relation to the state or the central government and the monarch. The reason for this appears to be the absence, or certainly the weakness, of the medieval system of monarchy, manor, and serf glued together by the Catholic church. In Scandinavia there were no serfs tied to the land. The bulk of the Scandinavian population were farmers or fisherfolk who owned their plots of land, however small, or who were self-employed. Naturally, there were some relatively large landowners of the manorial type, but farm workers and their families were not legally tied to the land. They could leave without permission, as thousands did, going to the United States from 1850 on. The state monarch had to bargain, as it were, with the local areas for taxes, military manpower, and other resources that the state monarch felt were needed for a respectable place among the emerging nation states of the Continent and England. Scandinavian monarchs were poor, but the early Swedish monarchs were especially ambitious.

The traditional county-state division of political and economic power had direct influence on the development of the Scandinavian health services in that counties became the major sources of Scandinavian health services finance and the loci of administration assisted and guided by the state. The health services delivery systems of the Scandinavian countries were characteristically a mixture of decentralization and centralization, both financial and administrative. Sweden's system appears to be more decentralized than the systems of its Scandinavian neighbors, and such decentralization is continuing. Among the countries selected for description and analysis here, Sweden moves clearly in the direction of market-minimized. Internationally, Sweden and the Swedish health services system have evoked a great deal of attention in other nations because of the country's low infant mortality rate, long life expectancy, high standard of living, advanced technology, and high-cost health care.

Among the Scandinavian countries, Sweden came to European attention during the early-seventeenth-century reign of Gustavus II. This king, known as Gustavus Adolphus, created a Swedish Baltic empire and maintained it successfully until his untimely death in battle in 1632, during the Thirty Years War on the Continent. The significance of Gustavus Adolphus's reign for the Swedish health services was that the war made Sweden a self-conscious national entity. The country consisted of a thousand or so small parishes. The monarch was rather poor to be embarking on empire building, but the Swedish farmers had many sons, a necessary resource for military exploits. Instead of taxes, the farmers provided sons. These young men came more or less from all over Sweden and returned more or less randomly. Many returned sons had contracted syphilis, which was then rampant on the Continent. The monarch, feeling some sense of national responsibility for this problem, subsidized selected parish-owned hospitals to care for the returning soldiers. They were called cure houses and were financed by a head tax on citizens over the entire country. They became known as crown hospitals.[1] One Swedish historian regarded the head tax as one form of sickness insurance in the government's fight against venereal disease.

In due course, and for obscure reasons, venereal disease receded, but the head tax remained as a primary source of funding for parish hospitals until the 1860s. After the end of the Napoleonic Wars, the Swedish monarchy and the government were left with a well-established and capable bureaucracy made up of "surplus" nobles who immigrated from the Continent. The bureaucracy then turned inward to develop the country economically. The government gradually became a parliamentary democracy, with the franchise extending to at least all the males. Sweden's economic resources, agriculture, forests, steel, and water power, if prudently managed, were eventually sufficient for a high standard of living. The Swedish health services naturally shared in the increasing social surplus.

The turning point, which had a great deal to do with the current structure of the Swedish health services, particularly the general hospital, was the amalgamation of the thousand or so parishes into 25 counties and four municipalities by an act of Parliament in 1862. The parishes were too small and too numerous to be an effective political counterweight to the central government and the king. The individual parishes had dealt directly with the king's representatives through a score or so of units called *län*, each with a governor appointed by the king to handle its local affairs. The farmers and the emerging middle class of merchants and professionals wanted a greater voice in the affairs of the government; they wanted locally elected representatives to the Parliament which was overloaded with aristocrats and big landowners. The Third Estate wanted more political power. The king, although a constitutional monarch, still exercised a great deal of power as a symbol. The overlapping of king and Parliament was legally clear enough, but the relationship was one of informal negotiation. (In time the monarchy became mainly a symbolic office above politics as an expression of national solidarity.)

The Parliament created new and larger political units, county councils, to replace the *län*. *Län* governors, however, continued to serve as the king's representatives in ceremonial matters. (The office of governor has become a prestigious position for retired politicians and civil servants.) Local political power was then in 1862 placed in elected representatives of the people in each of the newly created county councils according to political party affiliations. The county councils in turn elected representatives to the upper house in a two-chamber Parliament, thus facilitating some of the checks and balances characteristic of the liberal-democratic political philosophy. (Today there is only one chamber.)

1862–1955

After the county councils were established to diffuse power in the Parliament, there was some question as to what their function would be in addition to the purely political one. The state had been subsidizing selected parish hospitals. It was fully responsible for the public health officers throughout the country—local parishes could not support them. Through a political rationale difficult for even Swedish historians to evaluate, and stemming from the tradition of local hospital ownership and salaried physicians, the counties were given full ownership of the general hospitals and full fiscal and administrative responsibility. In 1864, the county councils received 20 percent of the retail tax on hard liquor collected by the state in the counties. A Swedish historian called this tax "sin money." The liquor tax was the financial backbone for the hospitals until the end of the nineteenth century; supplementary charges to patients were modest. This tax decreased, however, and was replaced by property and personal income taxes, which the state gave the counties power to raise.

It seems unlikely that the county councillors elected in 1862 realized the eventual magnitude of the responsibility the state had given them. The medical and scientific revolution had not yet occurred although, in Sweden as in all industrializing countries during the period, it was immediately imminent. Histories of some of the county councils reveal increasing concern with the rising cost of hospital care even then—for example, the x-ray machine was appearing. Surgery became more effective with anesthesiology and antisepsis. The situation of the county councils was unique because, outside of the municipalities, practically the only political issue with which the politicians had to deal was the one of establishing a hospital system good enough to vie with the systems of other counties. The hospital supply expanded rapidly in all counties. As a consequence, Sweden has the most hospital beds in relation to the population of any country in the world. This accounts for its continuing institutional emphasis, which the country is trying to reduce. On the other side, the state has been responsible for the supply of physicians by owning and financing the medical schools, literally deciding on the number of admissions. I infer that it was on the advice of the Swedish Academy of Medicine, not far from the Parliament House, that the physician supply in Sweden was held to the lowest ratio to population in the Western world until as late as the 1960s. Since then the physician supply has been expanded to exceed the ratio of that in Europe and North America. Thus, as early as 1862, and to a large extent earlier, the Swedish population had more or less free hospital care and the inpatient care of hospital-based physicians. In fact, in 1642, under Queen Christina, the hospitals were separated from the Poor Laws and made officially available to anyone, rich or poor—in short, they became community hospitals. (The Poor Laws were characteristic European methods—and carried over to the United States—to support people who were destitute; they provided that people who passed a means test could receive help from public sources.)

It is curious that this philosophy did not extend to out-of-hospital physician services until the legislation of 1947; it may be that free hospital care, including specialist services, inhibited the expansion of the range of service. In the meantime, the number of private practitioners of medicine outside the hospitals began to increase, and they struggled for private patients. As in other industrializing countries, many of these physicians were engaged by the workers' benefit associations that provided pensions and physician services through fees on workers and assistance from employers. It is likely that physician care for the poor outside the hospitals was provided by the parishes and by the noblesse oblige of the physicians, but it is also very likely that the poor had to be very sick indeed to receive treatment. Much later, in the twentieth century, voluntary health insurance for physician home and office services became quite common. Coverage varied, however, and voluntary insurance schemes did not become a political force to the extent they did in the United States.

As early as 1919 and through the 1930s, there were some political rumblings in the central government about having national health insurance for physician services, but nothing came of them until legislation was passed in 1947. The Swedish medical practitioners outside the hospitals were hardly enthusiastic about universal health insurance. Presumably, the hospital-based specialists were less concerned because they were already in the government system on the county level. Some of them had private practices on the side.

In the mid-1930s, the Social Democratic party came into power, ending the long reign of the Conservative party. The Social Democrats were a coalition of labor and farmers and remained in power until the late 1970s. During this period Sweden was transformed as an economic system into a welfare state by means of rather sophisticated negotiations among labor, management, and government. Production increased considerably, enabling the sharing of its largesse. Although the Social Democrats were regarded as socialists, they never reached the classic objective of socialism, that is, state ownership of the means of production and distribution. There were ideological divisions among the Social Democrats, and moderate pragmatists carried the day in that they were able to get the majority of the votes. It can be said that all Swedes are socialists but may be characterized as radical, moderate, or conservative. (It can also be said that all Americans are liberal, with their roots in British laissez faire liberalism, but may be characterized as radical, moderate, and conservative.)

After quite a number of years of government reports, discussions, and political debates, the universal physician insurance scheme was enacted in 1947. According to Swedish protocol, a law, although on the books, is not put into effect until the government decides to do so. There is an implementation period for consulting the parties at interest. The physician insurance law was put into effect in 1955. The eight-year interim was used by the government to negotiate administrative relationships and fees with the medical profession. About 600 sickness insurance agencies were set up by the government to be the paying agencies to the physicians outside hospitals and to pharmacies for certain life-saving medications. The government was the collection agency for deductions from employee paychecks and for contributions by employers, with some government contributions as well. Physicians were paid on a fee-for-service basis, up to three-quarters of their charges for general practitioners and 50 percent for specialists. Similar arrangements were made with hospital-based specialists for outpatient services in the hospital. There were no contracts as such with the sickness insurance agencies. The patients paid the balance and were reimbursed by the sickness insurance agencies. Pragmatic socialism is evident in that a charge or deductible at the time of service has not been a political issue to this day, or certainly not a serious one except among radical socialists.

Another government commission sat from 1943 to 1948 and reported one year after the passage of the physician insurance scheme. Presumably, this report was part of the discussion and debating process between the government and the physicians; it became known as the Höjer Report. Axel Höjer was the director general of the National Medical Board, which had national jurisdiction over medical standards and public health, among other matters. Höjer, a physician and a socialist, raised a furor among the medical profession by advocating a system of state medicine with salaried primary care physicians outside of hospitals. He believed that such an arrangement would integrate curative and preventive services, early diagnosis, and periodic health examinations.

Like the relative slowness of changes in public policy in general, the Swedish health services remained quite unchanged in structure and funding from 1862 to 1955. The greatest change, such as it was, took place in the private and voluntary sector for physician services through employer and employee benefit associations as fringe benefits. Despite the fact that Sweden did not have a public and comprehensive health service, the private and public sectors were becoming increasingly interrelated.

1955–1983

From 1955 on, the pace of change within the Swedish health services quickened, within the framework established between 1862 and 1955. General hospital services remained a county responsibility, and payment for physician services outside the hospital and for selected drugs became a central government responsibility in addition to the historical responsibility for public health officers and mental hospitals. Relief from onerous expenses on the part of the public was more important than an integrated service as envisioned by Höjer. Also, it is likely that payroll deductions for out-of-hospital physician services were more feasible if made by the central government than if made by the counties. Private production generated phenomenal growth in the gross national product, which enabled the financing of the welfare state pensions and other income redistributions.

Each county, however, was supposed to provide the full range of hospital services, from relatively simple inpatient care to complex care, and the increasingly high technology care became too expensive for many counties. This stimulated the idea of regionalizing hospital services. It made no sense for each county, regardless of size and resources, to own, finance, and operate a complete health system. By the late 1950s, the Federation of Swedish County Councils and the central government began to examine regionalization of hospitals. In 1958 a report was published recommending that Sweden be divided into seven regions, corresponding to the location of the seven medical schools with their associated high technology hospitals. These recommendations were based on rather detailed studies of population density, distance from hospitals, and distribution of hospitals by service capability conducted by a planning and research agency sponsored by the counties and central government and called the Swedish Planning and Rationalization Institute. (This agency is the central health services research data agency in Sweden and continually conducts studies in the health services.)

It appears that the formation of the regions was not a particularly politically charged endeavor. Seven counties were classified as having the full range of up-to-date technical medical services. Seventeen counties did not have the full range, although the majority did have technologically well-equipped hospitals. Counties contracted with the seven high-technology counties for services for their patients and transferred them to the high-technology centers. The formulation of the regions was made easier by the then director general of the National Medical Board, Arthur Engel. Engel was a physician, a former hospital administrator, a mediator, and a Conservative, just the opposite of his predecessor, Axel Höjer.

The reorganization was completed in 1960. The counties continued to have the usual financial responsibilities for hospitals, but the high-technology regional hospitals were financed in part by the central government for the portion of costs related to medical schools and teaching hospitals. In 1961, the government ceded to the counties the responsibility for all of the public health officers, who also practiced medicine. Later in 1961, the central government gave responsibility for the mental hospitals to the counties as well. And in 1971, the counties put public health officers on full salary. Note that the accumulating shift of responsibility for an increasing scope of services will lead incrementally, if it continues, to the type of health services structure that Höjer envisioned in 1948. The physicians paid on a fee-for-service basis outside the hospital were becoming more and more isolated from the mainstream. It seems to have been the Swedish political way to change the delivery of physician services without confronting the profession directly. This method is made easier because of the organizational split between the hospital-based specialists and the out-of-hospital general practitioners and specialists.

The hospital-based specialists, however, have not been left entirely undisturbed. Apparently not foreseen in 1955, when outpatient physician services came under universal insurance, was the much greater income that could be earned by laboratory physicians and radiologists and other specialists providing outpatient services in hospital clinics. With the new physician insurance scheme, the specialists were able to earn fees in addition to their salaries for inpatient services and to be paid by the sickness insurance agencies as were the out-of-hospital physicians. An unexpected development was the enormous increase in laboratory and radiology services that occurred as an aspect of changing medical practice. Laboratory physicians and radiologists paid by units of services were in many instances able to earn comparatively enormous incomes over their base salaries, with even the latter being high by Swedish standards.

The central government, which sets the salary levels in Sweden, began to negotiate early in 1969 with the hospital-based specialists and public health officers to abolish the outpatient fee system altogether and place everyone on full-time salary for both inpatient and outpatient services. Salaries would be graded but would ignore specialty differences. Until then surgeons, for example, were paid more than psychiatrists. Further, the specialists would have to provide service in the hospital clinics a precise number of hours per week rather than volunteer hours according to individual preference. The motive of the government was not so much to save money but to promote equity among specialists. It was not fair that one specialty should be paid more or less than another. The question was how to divide the existing pie of money for the hospital-based specialists. The specialists were split on this issue (making it easier for the government to deal with them), but they all regarded the move to establish hours of service as an interference with professional prerogatives. Was the hospital to become a factory with clock punching? Were the specialists to be paid for time they were on call, and so on?

The negotiations between the specialists and the government were intense and received wide press coverage. The specialists threatened withdrawal of service and only a short time before the deadline for the negotiations to be resolved was the deadlock ended. The professors in the medical schools received the highest settlement and no fixed hours in hospital. Of the 7,000 specialists at that time (1970), 1,700 came out with reduced incomes and the remainder with increased or unchanged incomes, but equity was established. The cost to the counties and the government remained the same. Furthermore, the government set aside a pool of money for three years for specialists whose incomes were to be reduced in order to lessen the effect of the reductions and to help the affected physicians with personal financial obligations during the time of transition. The fee system was eliminated for hospital-based specialists and public health officers and replaced with a full-time salary base. The patient, in turn, paid the deductible to the hospital rather than to the physician, who originally earned a fee for each outpatient service; the hospital collected the balance from the sickness insurance fund.

The private general practitioners and specialists outside the hospital paid by fees naturally began wondering if they would be the next to be salaried. In effect they were, because the government, in time, negotiated a fee schedule as full payment for the non-hospital-based physicians. These physicians then were not allowed the temptation to "extra bill" as in Canada until recently, and Australia and the United States currently. Further, since in a fee-for-service method of payment, physicians can in theory create their own demand, the Swedish government set a limit on the number of physician visits that the sickness insurance fund would reimburse in a year. The out-of-hospital physicians were then locked in as to both income limit and volume of services. Thus the counties and the government were set, as never before, to acquire greater control of the costs of the physician component of the Swedish health services. What remained relatively uncontrolled was the decision-making prerogatives of hospital-based specialists regarding the number of laboratory tests, x-rays, and high-technology procedures.

In the meantime, the total costs of the health services as a percentage of the gross national product increased, while Sweden faced a reduction in production and the erosion of foreign markets for products. What to do about the rapid rise in the cost of health services? The characteristic Swedish political style was to decentralize fiscal and operational responsibility. With this somewhat vague but persistent objective in mind, Sweden in 1976 established its first government commission on the Swedish health services. Before then the country had set up various commissions to ponder bits and pieces—outpatient services, maternal and child health, dental care, supply of personnel, and regionalization. For the first time a commission was to embrace the overall system.

The government commission set up in 1976 had an intentionally broad mission: to consider the legal framework of the working relationship between the central government and the counties. In an interview with the secretary of the commission, I asked if the commission would address the problem of rising costs. The answer was no because this was primarily the counties' problem to solve. I also asked him if the commission would consider the high supply of hospital beds. Again he said no, because supply was also a problem for the counties.

Instead, the commission directed its deliberation to generic policies of equal access, participatory democracy on all levels in the health services system, and decentralization of decision making all down the line. The commission reported in 1979.[2] The counties were given the formal responsibility with no timetable to assure all health services to all residents in one way or other. This meant not only personal health services but also control of environmental pollution and occupational diseases and injuries, and the health education of the public. The counties were also mandated to find ways of integrating health and social services, the latter having much to do with the elderly and their increasing numbers. The counties then became or were to become in effect by far the major source of funding for those global responsibilities and totally responsible for administration. In due time all out-of-hospital physician services and dental services are to come under the jurisdiction of the counties.

Perhaps even more radical than the foregoing shift is the January 1983 framework law (ramlag) which the central government has pushed over to the counties to implement. This directs that the government no longer specifies the hierarchical structure of the physicians and other personnel in the hospital, although the government still has the responsibility for training health services personnel, standards, and salary and wage levels. The Swedish authorities are very skittish about interfering with the professional prerogatives of diagnosis and treatment, but the new law approached this situation obliquely through the county—the point of delivery. The concept of participatory democracy is intended here in part to give greater balance of power to the nurses and technicians in relation to clinical decision making. The law created a legal atmosphere without the explicit regulations characteristic of American legalism.

The hierarchical structure did not have its basis in law, as it had previously, but in informal negotiation. Traditional hierarchies were abolished, and counties were to work out new ones. With this law, Sweden exhibited a remarkable cohesiveness of political values, a narrow consensus as to what as a matter of course is fair and right. The law itself was not coercive in a direct sense, but if informal norms and customs can be worked out they can in practice be just as coercive.

What I read into this new law, although there appears to be no explicit interpretation among Swedish policymakers, is that the government had despaired of controlling the rising costs of health services centrally and had, therefore, given almost the entire responsibility to the counties, traditional custodians of the bulk of health services expenditures—the hospitals since 1862 and additional components of services since. It should be noted that the new law was not particularly politically controversial. It had multiparty support. The policy was congenial to the decentralization and participatory democratic trends of the country; it placed fiscal and administrative responsibility for health services as close to the people as possible. The people are presumably closer to the county politicians than to the central government. There are no strong citizens groups to badger the health services delivery system inside the government structure. In a sense, in Sweden the state and society are more or less the same, and the state is not regarded as another interest group. Continuing expansion of the health services, however, seems to be inherent in the previous implicit policies of the country on the part of the counties and the previous expansion policies of the government. A report from the Federation of County Councils, for example, anticipates continuing expansion.[3]

Still, the director of planning for the county of Stockholm (which includes the city) reported in 1983 a great deal of dissatisfaction in Sweden from many directions.[4] He wrote that planners were being besieged by patient associations, politicians, and committees of Parliament. They were alienating the "technical planners"—the professionals—who operate with advanced systems hard to understand by the groups mentioned above. Distrust was increasing. There are feelings and options that cannot be programmed for a computer, such as quality of life. Averages will not be accepted in the face of horror stories; though incidents are infrequent, the mass media publicize them.

1983–1986

In the wake of all this, there has been emerging interest in what is called in Canada, Great Britain, and the Scandinavian countries privatization, that is, the use of some market-oriented methods to control the costs of health services. That privatization emerged in Sweden as a subject for possible examination and discussion for policymaking is a remarkable phenomenon. In the years since 1951 I have engaged in research trips to Great Britain and Scandinavia (annually from 1958 to 1979), but I did not foresee the possibility of such public discussion and debate. Privatization was a nonissue and ideologically impious. In 1984 the department of social medicine at Uppsala University sponsored a seminar on the subject.[5] The first brochure on the subject, with many qualified contributors, came out in 1985 and was sponsored by the Swedish Planning and Rationalization Institute.[6] It is evident that the discussions and debates were then in an early stage—privatization was a new subject and in part an unthinkable one. The issues were posed as either/or, private health care or public health care, cooperation or competition. In time, it is likely that the subtleties and complexities of the relationships of the private and public sectors will be recognized in an economy that is already mixed. It is of interest that at this time the United States is a reference point for having the kernel of a method to contain cost escalation, rather than the usual reference point for inequities and wastefulness.

The emerging evidence is that Scandia, a private insurance company, is selling health insurance to employees through their employers. There are increasing allegations that waiting lists are growing for elective surgery such as cataract operations and lens replacements and also hip replacements. In fact, a private clinic has been established by doctors to provide faster walk-in service and services for elective surgery. The chairman of the Stockholm County Council, an elected official, believed that waiting lists could be made an election issue.[7]

Summary

The question of privatization aside, the law that went into effect in January 1983 gave the counties nearly total responsibility for the ownership, operation, and financing of the entire health services establishment. In this way, Sweden ushered in the era of management and control. Nevertheless, Sweden is increasingly distressed by the fact that costs continue to rise. Decentralization does not appear to be the hoped-for panacea. Like all countries, Sweden is learning that personal health services are intrinsically expensive if a country wishes to keep up with technological advances in medicine and with equality of access. Because of the decentralized nature of its health services financing and administrative responsibility, Sweden is placed immediately to the right of the United Kingdom in the market-mini-mized/market-maximized continuum.

Notes

1. The history of the Swedish health services is drawn from Odin W. Anderson, *Health Care: Can There be Equity? The United States, Sweden and England* (New York: John Wiley & Sons, 1972). The history is rather thoroughly documented in this book until 1970. Those who want specific references should consult it. They are too voluminous to include in this short chapter. Further developments in the Swedish health service since 1970 will be documented in some detail.
2. Landstingsförbundet, *Nya Hälso-och Sjukvård slag for Utveckling av Hälso-och Sjukvården* (Stockholm: Landstingsförbundet, 1982) is a description of the law that emanated from the Government Commission Report. There was also a rela-tively short simple report for the public. The Swedish people could hardly com-plain about being inadequately informed if they read the information available. The mass media are also helpful.
3. Landstingsförbundet, *Budgetstatistik for Landstingen 1983, med Utgifts och In-komsprognos for 1982 och 1983* (Stockholm: Landstingsförbundet, LKELP83, Rapport No. 1, 1982).
4. Ulf Zetterblad, "Health Care in the County of Stockholm," *World Hospitals* 19 (April 1983): 51–54.
5. Reported in the Journal of the Swedish Medical Association, *Läkartidningen* 81, No. 45 (1984): 4131–36, 4142–44.
6. Egon Jonsson and Douglas Skalin, eds., *Privat och Offentlig Sjukvård, Samverkan el/er Konkurrens* (Stockholm: Sjukvårdens och Socialvårdens Planerings-och Raitonaliseringsinstitut, 1985).
7. Interview in Stockholm, August 1986.

Chapter 5

Canada

Before 1945

Like the United States and Australia, Canada is a federation of relatively autonomous states. Its ten provinces share powers under the Constitution of 1867 with the dominion government. Health and welfare fall within the jurisdiction of the provinces. Canada, again like the United States and Australia, became increasingly a national entity that needed more cooperative relationships between the center and the provinces on the locus of taxing powers and kinds of taxes. The central government grew powerful fiscally because it in large part preempted personal and corporate income tax prerogatives. In a federation, then, a major source of funding became the federal government, but the major locus of spending for health and welfare services remained with the provinces. Over time, some provinces became relatively rich, and some became relatively poor. The emergence of egalitarian values directed the federal government to be an equalizing agent so that disparities—particularly those in health services and welfare—among provinces would be minimized.

Carl Meilicke and Janet Storch divide the political and economic development of Canada into five periods: (1) preconfederation (to 1867); (2) confederation to the mid-1940s; (3) the mid-1940s to the mid-1960s; (4) the mid-1960s to the mid-1970s, and (5) the future.[1] Health and welfare policy evolved as a national concern and affected greatly the fiscal relationships between the federal government and the provinces. Canadian provinces seem to be even more self-conscious political entities than the American states. Regionally, the country divides itself into the Western provinces and the Eastern provinces, with Ontario and Quebec as political swing provinces. The differences in wealth and population magnitudes are great, as are differences in cultural styles. The province of Quebec, a French-speaking social and cultural entity is a case in point. (This province will be described separately because how it relates to the federal government, its fiscal arrangements, and its internal health and welfare policies differ from those of other provinces.)

It took until the end of Meilicke and Storch's second era (confederation to the mid-1940s) before bureaucrats and politicians at the national level in Ottawa felt able to conceive a national health and welfare policy and to interrelate provincial and federal prerogatives and responsibilities. It seems reasonable to observe that national leadership at this time, during the Second World War, came forward because of the total mobilization of the economic and human resources of the country for a common objective. There was a great deal of wartime euphoria holding the country together to build a better postwar world with liberty and distributive justice to create protection from unemployment, pensions in old age, and health services for all. Two major reports emerged from the federal government during this time. The Marsh Report on social security for Canada and the Heagerty Report of the advisory committee on health insurance. Both reports formed the basis for the Dominion-Provincial Conference on Reconstruction in 1945 to consider national unemployment compensation, old-age pensions, and health insurance. To add to the euphoria, Sir William Beveridge, the British author of the famous Beveridge Plan to eliminate poverty, ignorance, and squalor in the postwar world flew over from England to lend his support. The Canadian Medical Association, the Canadian Hospital Council, and the Canadian Life Insurance Office Association all supported universal health insurance in principle, given certain conditions.

Then came the postwar return to more mundane, routine problems than fighting a war. The political self-determination of the provinces resurfaced, and national leadership became muted. From the mid-1940s to the mid-1960s, there were major developments in social security policy and programs at both the federal and provincial levels, but Meilicke and Storch complain of "disjointed incrementalism." The order in which new programs were established was not guided by a "formal rational plan" as had been conceived by the Marsh and Heagerty reports and the Dominion-Provincial Conference. The relatively loose federalism of the Canadian system meant that power was flowing back to the provinces. The problem was how to structure what would be seen by both the dominion and the provinces as an equitable sharing of fiscal responsibilities in a system where the federal government had most of the money and the provinces did most of the spending.

As far as universal health insurance was concerned, the province of

Saskatchewan was regarded as an exception from other provinces and the federal government in setting forth a planned health services delivery system and health insurance. The action by this province became a reference point for other provinces and led to a national system, the development of which occupies the rest of this chapter.[2]

Canada, the United States, and Australia have remarkably similar health services delivery structures, ones to which prepayment mechanisms were grafted. Canada has freestanding community hospitals, many of them voluntary and started by community boards or church denominations, and autonomous physicians practicing in their own offices and paid on a fee-for-service basis. The physicians apply to hospitals for the privilege of admitting their patients. This structure was in place by the 1930s, thus preceding the stage of third-party payers, both private and public. This pattern existed in all provinces. It is on this health services delivery structure that Canadian provinces and, later, through a national plan, that Canada built its provincial- federal health insurance edifice.

Historical provincial autonomy appeared to inhibit federal initiatives, just as was true in the United States before the Social Security Act of 1935 and in Australia into the 1940s. As early as 1919, the Liberal party in Canada put health insurance in its platform. In 1930, as health insurance became a more popular political issue, Saskatchewan initiated catastrophic insurance for cancer, expanding it in 1944. Alberta in 1944 got as far as enacting a maternity hospital plan.

After the Dominion-Provincial Conference's failure to agree to the reallocations of tax resources, any province that wanted to "go it alone," as was the usual expression, could do so, using its own resources. It turned out that Saskatchewan, which was hardly the most prosperous province, became the cradle for a socialistically oriented party called the Canadian Commonwealth Federation (CCF). Saskatchewan started to go it alone before the demise of the Dominion-Provincial Conference. In 1945, after the CCF came into power, the province decided to embark on a provincial health insurance plan.

As usual such an event has a history. From roughly 1914 through the 1930s, because Saskatchewan was sparsely settled and the population lived on a single crop, wheat, the province established for a large minority of the farmers an arrangement called the "municipal doctor system." To attract doctors, the provincial legislature granted authority to rural municipal councils to levy taxes. Since doctors could not earn enough by fees for services because of the low population density (not necessarily because of poverty), the municipal doctor system paid them a retainer to help them get established, and they charged fees as well. Authority to establish these arrangements was later extended to villages and towns.

Paralleling these arrangements, the provincial government of Saskatchewan empowered towns, villages, and rural municipalities to establish joint hospital systems called unions. By 1947, there were 78 unions covering a third of the settled area of the province. The new CCF government in 1945 provided grants for hospital construction through these units.

These developments for promoting the availability of hospitals and physicians were part of a basic movement in Saskatchewan of producer cooperatives among the wheat farmers to have some control over marketing their grain. These cooperatives were more extensive than in any other province in Canada. Similar marketing problems also produced cooperatives among farmers in the Dakotas, Minnesota, and Wisconsin in the United States. This form of collectivism seemed to be congenial to the creation of the CCF. It is of interest, however, to note that collectivism never seemed to evolve in the direction of classical socialism for the people through the state to own and operate the means of production and distribution. It is unlikely that farmers were that collectivistic; they only wanted to control their markets much as other producers. The health and welfare services, however, were the first and fair game to socialize in the public interest; hence, government health insurance became the first objective and hospitals and physicians the first targets. The strategy, however, became one of first insuring hospital services—a public concern because they were becoming more and more expensive.

Saskatchewan the Leader: 1945

The CCF actually built on the political debate on health insurance started by the incumbent Liberals in Saskatchewan during World War II. The Liberals had been in power for many years when the CCF came in in 1944. In brief, the Liberal party, with the expectation that the federal government after the war would initiate some sort of federal-provincial health insurance scheme, passed a law hastily in 1944 to get ready for the possibility. Two-and-one-half years later the CCF government enacted the first universal hospital service plan in North America. Malcolm Taylor lists the following reasons for CCF government action: (1) an inadequate number of hospital beds and physicians; (2) the perceived inadequacies of the municipal hospital plans; (3) the generally favorable political climate; and (4) personal and political party commitment.[3] The political leadership was not hesitant; it seemed to know what it wanted and was not waiting for a diverse assortment of pressure groups, and the providers were not hostile to the idea.

The implementation of the hospital insurance plan in Saskatchewan was preceded by studies and action once there was political consensus for legislation. There was a lack of experts in the health department, but those who were appointed had ability and deep sympathy for the objectives, and other temporary experts, such as Professor Henry Sigerist, were imported from the Johns Hopkins University medical school to conduct a survey of general resources, facilities, and personnel and how they might be structured. The result on paper was the standard package of public health philosophy; regionalization; and classification of facilities by acute, chronic, convalescent, and free hospital care, since the emphasis of the legislation was the hospital.

The consultant's report received a good deal of publicity and provided the government with a rough sketch rather than a blueprint. The permanent technical staff could work out the details. The staff in short order began drafting a health services act to (1) create a health services planning commission to be appointed by the government and (2) authorize the minister for public health to pay part or all of the cost of providing health services for such classes of people as the government might designate. This was done.

From there on, it seemed that the implementation of the hospital insurance act became mainly a technical problem to devise methods of classifying and paying hospitals and methods and kinds of statistical record keeping and sources of funding. It was decided that the provincial government should contribute from general revenue. Fred Mott, a U.S. doctor with a degree from McGill University and extensive experience with rural health services and prepayment in the United States, became the first director of the commission. While I was visiting him in Regina in 1948, he said that Saskatchewan was learning how to pay hospitals. There was no particular concern with how much hospitals were used. Increased access was a goal, and the hospital supply was expanded considerably to achieve the highest bed-to-population ratio and the greatest use in North America.

In addition to the hospital insurance plan, the health services planning commission set up demonstration projects in two areas of the province, Swift Current and Weyburn, to integrate hospital, physician, and public health services. In due course, however, there was a consensus that a provincewide hospitalization program should have the highest priority. The two areas mentioned, particularly Swift Current, became well known as models for physician services prepayment and primary care. Saskatchewan then became the reference point for health insurance for other provinces and the federal government, despite what those entities saw as its socialistic tinge. The Saskatchewan experience assuaged fears elsewhere that hospital insurance was unworkable and too costly. By all usual standards it worked. Hospitals prospered, the public was not faced with large hospital bills, and physicians could recommend admission as medically indicated. Observers from other provinces and the federal government came to Saskatchewan to see for themselves, thus hastening the learning and diffusion process and the eventual enactment of a national hospital insurance program. The political process leading to national hospital insurance, however, was turbulent.

Shift to National Debate: Hospital Insurance

The continuing Liberal government in Ottawa was historically committed to some form of universal health insurance, but it wobbled on the issues of how to share costs with the provinces, the extent of interference with provincial administrative details, and the extent of coverage. Ontario decided not to go it alone, but to wait for signals from the federal level to participate in funding. British Columbia, however, did enact a hospital insurance program in 1948, with a rather rocky implementation experience because of lack of advanced planning, inadequate time for training of new staff, and two complicated collection systems.

A national political consensus was emerging that Canada should not "balkanize" its health insurance by allowing it to develop in the provinces without federal coordination for standards of benefits and equity. Despite the fact that the federal-provincial political discussion appeared to embrace health insurance in general rather than hospital insurance in particular, it seemed—with Saskatchewan's emerging experience, the apparent desires of the public, and the apparent support of the Canadian Medical Association—that hospital insurance would be politically expedient.

The conventional wisdom among medical care experts was that starting with hospitals was an exceedingly unwise strategy for launching a universal health insurance program, since it emphasized the most expensive component of the service spectrum. As Taylor observed, it is easy with hindsight to argue that a different sequence of introducing various components of service should have been planned, such as starting with preventive services. He writes that it should be recalled that hospital bills were the hardest ones for families to pay, hospitals were in bad fiscal shape, and voluntary health insurance in Canada had already established patterns to which providers and the public were accustomed. In short, it seemed important to get something started and then work toward a more logical system from there.[4]

It took ten years of federal financial discussions and debates to hammer out the federal-provincial fiscal and administrative relationships for hospital insurance. In the meantime, an interesting transformation was taking place in Canadian health insurance: Canadian hospitals and physicians were coming to regard voluntary health insurance in the United States as a reference point; they could generate similar schemes in Canada as a counterpoint to government insurance.

Ten years gave the Canadian hospitals and medical profession, particularly the latter, time to develop their own version of Blue Shield and Blue Cross plans. To what extent these plans were in direct response to the universal health insurance debate in the United States is not easy to determine, but it seems to be clear that once these plans got started, they grew more rapidly than even their sponsors anticipated. In 1947, voluntary health insurance in Canada was hardly visible. Ten years later, the provincial medical societies had established their own prepayment plans in most provinces, and in 1957 they established a national coordinating agency called the Trans-Canada Medical Plan for national accounts. The medical profession began to sense an alternative to government, as did other interests such as the commercial insurance companies and business groups. A solution would be government responsibility for the poor, as was traditional, or enrolling the poor in voluntary insurance plans subsidized by government. The profession feared the "entering wedge" of universal hospital insurance and the inclusion of radiologists and pathologists.

The consensus for a nationwide hospital insurance scheme gained momentum. Federal-provincial fiscal and administrative relationships were hammered out by constant discussions. On April 10, 1957, to "tumultuous applause," the House voted 165 to 0 for the scheme. Two days later the Senate did the same. Acrimonious debates finally resulted in an enthusiastic consensus, the hallmark of a vital liberal democracy.

Taylor believes that the degree of control the provinces accepted from the federal government was extraordinary since the federal government prescribed all essential details for the operation of the program. But the access to generous federal cost sharing afforded provinces by the arrangement was too tempting to resist. The provinces had to establish hospital planning divisions; they had to license, inspect, and supervise hospitals and have them maintain certain standards; they had to approve hospital budgets; they had to make insured services available to all on uniform terms and conditions. By 1962 even Quebec had joined, and the scheme became nationwide. The usual ownership pattern of hospitals remained, an amalgam of private ownership and public subsidy, an arrangement typical of a mixed-economy liberal democracy.

Saskatchewan Physician Insurance

Saskatchewan, which already had a hospital insurance scheme, suddenly found that it could be relieved of one-half the cost of hospital care, with the balance to come from the federal treasury, to which, of course, Saskatchewan residents contributed. The only way that the province could get its contribution back, however, was to join the national scheme, and it did so gladly. The resulting cost sharing with the federal government provided the province with at least a paper surplus and enabled it to start seriously considering moving to physician insurance—insurance to cover the costs of physician services. By this time also, in the late 1950s, Saskatchewan was no longer a poor province; it was a national and even worldwide breadbasket and not the drought-stricken area of the 1930s.

Taking on the physicians, however, turned out to be a very different experience. By this time, the physicians also were prosperous, and the profession had established two prepayment plans of its own, as had the medical societies in the other provinces. The physicians had an alternative to the CCF's Swift Current model of comprehensive services, fee schedules, and a trend toward a salaried service.

In Saskatchewan, the College of Physicians and Surgeons combined two functions in the same organization: the self-regulation of professional standards and looking after the profession's economic interests. The college had a strong position relative to the government and presented the standard and predictable counterproposals in response to the equally standard and predictable proposals of the CCF government. The college held that, should there be a physician insurance plan, it should be administered by a commission rather than by a department of the government. This proposal was based on the assumption that a commission made up of a spectrum of interests including physicians could be more insulated from direct political influences (as if a public service such as health service could really be nonpartisan). Another stipulation was that physicians should be paid through an intermediary, with their own prepayment plans acting as that intermediary. There should be freedom of choice of location to practice, freedom of patient choice of physician, freedom for physicians to choose whether or not to participate in an insurance plan, and freedom for physicians to determine the method of remuneration.

These stipulations, of course, flew in the face of the ability and right of citizens, through their elected representatives, to determine the methods, amounts, and sources of payments for health services and the structures for delivering care. The profession, of course, had the right to negotiate and bargain like any other group, but its stipulations amounted to an ultimatum. The college did, however, have supporters from the Liberal party, the chamber of commerce, and pharmaceutical and dental associations, based on the fear of general socialization. In essence the college wanted an arrangement whereby voluntary health insurance would be the main vehicle for the self-supporting public, with private subsidy for low-income persons and other segments of the population that were inherently difficult to cover in a private system.

A physician insurance scheme was passed, despite the physicians' adamant and united opposition, in the fall of 1961. The College of Physicians and Surgeons claimed that it was not consulted sufficiently before the passage of the act. The government, however, had given in to a representative commission form of administration and felt that politically it could not delay enactment any longer: already the political timetable was delayed nine months. Implementation *was* delayed further, though, as the government and college negotiated during what became a bitter strike of the physicians. The three-week strike took place on a single issue of importance to the profession, that the physicians be allowed to bill the patient directly if they wished or to bill the commission set up by the province to pay claims sent in by the physicians. This stipulation, of course, would erode government control over physician fees, since by billing the patient directly the physicians would not be bound by the fee ceiling. The government felt rightly that the College of Physicians and Surgeons was denying the government's ability to direct the development of the Saskatchewan health services toward regionalization, salaried physicians, and the integration of preventive and curative services.

In the end, the government gave the medical profession the option of being paid through the physician-controlled plans as well as through the commission and granted the plans the authority to act as insurers for a variety of supplementary benefits. Otherwise, the people of Saskatchewan were universally covered, and the scheme was tax-supported. The government gave up the possibility of developing a regionalized system of health services, and the agreement perpetuated in substance the traditional preferences of the medical profession. As far as the public was concerned, it was freed of onerous medical bills; the cost barrier had been removed. In fact, the public's fear of extra billing by physicians stimulated the growth of the voluntary prepayment plans. Methods of organization at that time were mainly the interest of health services organization experts.

The National Debate over Physician Insurance, 1962

Thus, Saskatchewan again became a reference point, this time for physician insurance. Three provinces—British Columbia, Alberta, and Ontario—proposed physician insurance plans that conformed to the desires of the medical profession and the insurance industry, and, because the Canadian health insurance system was incomplete, a federal physician insurance scheme became a viable political issue.

At the request of the Canadian Medical Association, the federal government convened a royal commission on health services known as the Hall Commission, Emmett M. Hall being a well-respected judge from Saskatchewan. The commission's 1964 report, a thorough and voluminous one, recommended, in effect, a universal, federal-provincial, comprehensive health insurance system, with the federal government to enter into agreements with the provinces to provide grants based on a fiscal-need formula. The report also emphasized the need to set "uniform terms and conditions" for the entire population, thus rejecting the policy of a subsidy for the poor proposed by the Canadian Medical Association and its supporters. The means test was regarded not only as demeaning, but also as impractical to administer. The report supported the concept of a basic service, free choice of physician and hospital, and free choice of additional items that could be insured through private insurance.

Again, on the federal-provincial level as in Saskatchewan, there was a great deal of debate, but not about the reorganization of the personal health services or even universality. This time the dispute centered on how the provinces and the federal government should share the costs and to what extent the federal government should prescribe the details of provincial administration and operation. Taylor observes that by this time the provinces had seven years of experience with the hospital insurance program and would not tolerate the formal agreements and detailed federal auditing of provincial accounts.[5] What the provinces wanted was a plan based on a general understanding of the principles of a health insurance program. They feared excessive technical legalisms on the part of a powerful central government with an enormous taxing power. Certainly, the essence of a liberal-democratic government is trust between adversaries and among interest groups, and the law and its rules and regulations form a framework for cooperation.

The elegant outcome of the intense but still civil hassling among these interest groups was that the principles of federal-provincial cooperation were reduced to an absolute minimum of four: (1) comprehensive services, (2) universality, (3) administration by public agencies, and (4) portability, that is, individuals' coverage should be transferable from province to province. If the provinces agreed to these principles, they could receive grants from the federal government for hospital and physician services. The provinces would become the sole negotiators with the providers, and administration would be decentralized to them, along with partial responsibility for financing. The federal government would provide roughly one-half of the money. The first principal, comprehensive services, meant hospital and physician services. The provinces were free to add other services at their own expense; they could organize services and pay providers in any way they wished. It is of interest, however, that in the course of events the traditional structure of the service delivery system remained intact. Saskatchewan had shown the dangers of forcing physicians into patterns they did not desire. The province of Quebec took a different direction from the other provinces—a story in itself, as will be shown in due course.

What became Medicare in Canada became law in December 1966. Not until January 1971, however, was Medicare in operation in all the provinces. This is because the provinces had the option of joining the federal plan or not. The grants to the provinces were, of course, a powerful temptation, but only Saskatchewan and British Columbia met the principles on the inaugural date. The pivotal provinces of Ontario and Quebec came into the federal plan in October 1969 and November 1970, respectively. The last province, New Brunswick, qualified in January 1971.

The foregoing description of a seemingly smooth introduction of a national physician insurance plan in tandem with the hospital insurance plan belies an intensive and rigorous political battle too detailed to present in this book. Changes in government in Ottawa meant differences in the degree of enthusiasm for a national health insurance plan, but the Liberals were committed historically and played for proper political timing. The Canadian Medical Association and its supporters wanted voluntary health insurance to be the major health insurance vehicle for the employed segment of the population, with subsidies to the poor. They were cheered by the rapid increase in the various forms of prepayment, medical society and hospital-sponsored plans, and commercial insurance.

Health insurance became a fringe benefit to be negotiated between labor and management. A clear majority of the population was covered by private hospital and medical insurance. The overriding equity issue, however, transcended the accomplishments of private insurance companies. Private insurance did not cover the self-employed, those with low incomes, the unemployed, or the elderly, nor did it solve the problem of adequate distribution of hospitals and physicians. These are common criticisms in all countries that started, in the main, with voluntary private insurance. What was worse, the existing benefits were inadequate; they did not really cover catastrophic illnesses. Only a universal, governmental scheme could correct the deficiencies.

The Canadian philosophy of public accountability, it is relevant to note, precluded the government from contracting for health services by private administrative intermediaries. This principle was apparently strong enough to sanction the destruction of flourishing enterprises, such as the Blue Cross and Blue Shield plans. Australian and U.S. political philosophy would be quite reluctant to see this happen, if for no other reason than to prevent the growth of a large public bureaucracy. In any case, voluntary plans existing at the time of the enactment of Canadian Medicare set up insurance to pay for health services not covered by Medicare, for example, dental services, private rooms in hospitals, and medications. Private insurance for services already covered by Medicare was forbidden. After an account of the actions in the province of Quebec, I discuss the policy issues that surfaced in the years after Canada adopted a federal-provincial physician insurance scheme.

The Province of Quebec

The negotiation between the province of Quebec and the federal government on the hospital insurance scheme was relatively calm, helped along by the fact that the federal government permitted Quebec to fund its plan indirectly from federal funds by manipulating the income tax on corporations. In Quebec's view, this arrangement softened the conditions under which the province complied with the four principles, although there was apparent satisfaction with them. The province wished to maintain as much fiscal independence from the federal government as possible, at least symbolically. By the 1960s, however, Quebec had become increasingly desirous of complete independence, short of withdrawal from the federation (and there was a vigorous and visible minority agitating for this), to run its own domestic affairs in a manner approaching that of a sovereign country. In 1966, when the federal government was proposing another conditional grant program, the province wished to set up its own health insurance program in its own way and from the perspective of its own philosophy of a good society.

The general welfare-state philosophy emerging in Quebec, although coming later than in some other provinces, seems not to have been basically different from that of Canada as a whole.[6] The shape Quebec's health insurance was taking, however, differed from the pattern that other provinces were accepting, given Saskatchewan's failed attempt to establish a planned, regionalized, provincial system with health centers and salaried physicians. Quebec envisioned just such a rationalized system. This vision did not preclude accepting the four principles of the federal government's proposal, but Quebec was caught between two forces: the external pressure of the federal government and the internal pressure of the medical specialists supported by big business, industry, and the Canadian Medical Association. Early in 1966 a Liberal government set up a research committee, chaired by actuary Claude Castonguay, to begin investigations of health services and insurance in the province. A change of government in the middle of that year, to the Union Nationale party (sympathetic to separation), did not bring a change in strategy. The new government appointed a commission of inquiry in November 1966, with Claude Castonguay again as the chair.

A national precedent had already been set in 1964 with the report of the Hall Commission, which boldly recommended a provincially administered national scheme of physician insurance paralleling hospital insurance. The Castonguay Report released in 1967 was even bolder in documenting the relative inequities of health services and health conditions in Quebec, and in recommending not only universal health insurance, with acceptance of the four principles, but also the forbidding of physicians to

opt out of the system and still be paid for services to patients. This requirement applied to specialists only, for the association of general practitioners
was in favor of universal health insurance in principle. In Quebec, unlike
other provinces, specialists were largely hospital-based, and general practitioners did not have hospital admission privileges along the British and
Continental patterns. Over time, the specialists had acquired great autonomy and power over resources and fee-charging prerogatives. Physician
services in Quebec had not been covered by health insurance in any form
until a relatively late date, compared with the other provinces, because
private health insurance was not as extensive and physicians had not developed their own prepayment schemes. Exposure to the complexities of health
insurance, and then a plan mandated by government, was a new experience
for the physicians and very threatening.

The power of the specialists became evident in the summer of 1967
when, under the hospital insurance program, 205 radiologists withdrew all
but emergency services. In September, they were supported by 2,300 specialists who refused to participate any longer in the social assistance medical
plan for the poor. The government relented and agreed to pay for radiology
services in private offices and to authorize a general increase in fees.

The Union Nationale government in 1970 introduced a health insurance bill that received unanimous approval at first reading and that gave no
comfort to the specialists. It proposed universal, comprehensive, portable
insurance to be administered by the Health Insurance Board. It differed from
the other provincial plans in two basic respects: it would be financed by a
0.8 percent income tax and by a 0.8 percent tax on employers. The provision that affected the specialists, however, held that physicians could opt
out, but that, if they did so, their patients would not be reimbursed for any
portion of their fees. When the Liberals came back into power, with Castonguay as minister of health, they proposed a bill making one concession: a
maximum of 3 percent of the physicians in any specialty and 3 percent of
the physicians in any administrative region would be permitted to opt out
and have their patients reimbursed up to a maximum of 75 percent of the
established fee schedule. A new proposal also called for a five-member
board to resolve disputes between physicians and the Health Insurance
Board, with two physician members.

Not surprisingly, the specialists attacked the 3-percent limitation, as-
serting that all physicians should have the right to opt out and yet have their
patients reimbursed. They also were very critical of the five-member board
to resolve disputes, insisting that all aspects of practice should remain under
the control of the College of Physicians and Surgeons. An equally strong
protest came from the unions of labor, teachers, and farmers, who wanted a
British-style system of state medicine and salaried physicians and a break in
the traditional and entrenched power of organized medicine. The govern-

ment, with strong general public support, continued to seek passage of a universal plan by July 1, 1970.

The unions threatened to strike if the opting-out provision were kept in; the specialists said they would not sign an agreement if the provision were not substantially expanded. In addition, the profession perceived three other provisions as flying in the face of highly valued prerogatives: (1) the loss of opportunity to deal financially directly with the patient rather than with the government insurance system and to charge fees above the government rates, a practice allowed in other provinces; (2) the removal of control of strictly professional matters from the College of Physicians and Surgeons and the transfer of that control to the Health Insurance Board; and (3) an anticipated reduction in income because of predicted insufficient appropriations to the insurance fund.

The provincial government feared that the freedom to opt out would add considerably to the cost for the public and, at the same time, feared an exodus of the most highly qualified specialists from the province. According to Taylor, the government came to the conclusion that in the long run it would rather risk an exodus than permit a general opting out of the program.[7] The opting-out clause remained in the final bill, with the proviso that the patients of physicians who did opt out could not be reimbursed by the insurance fund.

The bill was passed by a large majority, and the contending parties squared off. Quebec specialists voted in favor of a resolution that in effect meant a strike. The government held fast on the opting-out issue but decided to increase the health insurance fund to permit higher fees. On October 8, the specialists began a full-fledged strike, maintaining emergency services in only 38 hospitals; many specialists had left the province.

Another emergency, however, transcended that of the specialists' strike. The British Trade Commissioner had been kidnapped on October 5 and was being held for a very high ransom by one of the Quebec separatist cells. A few days later, the Labour Minister was kidnapped by a different cell. The army was ordered to guard important buildings and individuals in Ottawa, 100 miles away. The specialists offered a conditional truce and were seen as taking advantage of the extreme public emergency. The government refused their offer, and the Quebec Hospital Association, the Association of Medical Directors, and the Association of French Language Doctors ordered the specialists to call off the strike. The College of Physicians and Surgeons urged an immediate end to the strike, and the opposition Parti Quebecois appealed for an immediate return to work. Ominously, one of the separatist cells threatened to kidnap a physician if the strike did not end.

The National Assembly authorized health insurance—now Medicare—to start November 1 whether or not the specialists agreed and ordered the specialists back to work. The federal government, at the request of the

Quebec government, invoked the War Measures Act, outlawing the Front de Libération de Quebec and suspending normal due process governing "search, arrest, and detention."

Despite all appeals, the specialists held to their position. Two days later, however, sobered by the news of the murder of the Labour Minister, with demonstrations in the streets expected and with panic among the public, "they saw that the time had come to end the strike and obey the law."[8] They decided to return under protest. On November 1, 1970—4 months behind its own schedule and 24 months behind the Ottawa schedule—the Quebec Medicare program began to operate. The government was credited with bringing the profession to heel. The extent to which the kidnapping crisis and the invocation of the War Measures Act were the main reasons for the capitulation of the specialists is an interesting matter for speculation. Could the government have won unconditionally without the crisis atmosphere? In no other government-profession showdown had the government won so completely. Medicare was now a national program.

Curiously, the Medicare legislation in Quebec set up a fairly elaborate regional system, as described by Roger Gosselin and Victor Rodwin.[9] The Castonguay Commission and in 1970 the Castonguay-Nepveu Commission recommended the formation of regional councils that would be vested with strong executive powers within each of the three large regions making up the province of Quebec. The recommendations aimed at decentralizing the management of services, creating regional bodies within which interested parties would participate in establishing priorities, formulating programs, allocating resources, and assessing program efficiency and effectiveness. The councils were to involve local people in taking a holistic approach to health issues, considering physical, behavioral, and social factors. The various interests should negotiate and make "deals," by persuasion and goodwill. The councils had no power to raise money; that power resided in the central government. They were to become increasingly responsible for planning and to accept or reject all renovations and plans for expansion submitted by the providers. The government would take over the financing and direct control of the hospitals, including those owned by the Catholic church. (The church hospitals had for years been running steep deficits, which had been made up by the provincial treasury.)

The commission recommendations also established, through the councils, health centers that would incorporate primary and preventive services. It is curious that the specialists did not make an issue of this potential control over the profession. They probably did not feel they were involved, at least not in the immediate future, although the general practitioners were fearful of being herded into the health centers. In any case, the health centers gradually increased in number (to 150 to 1986), and there is a provincial federation of health centers. But their number will probably not be large, for physicians themselves are setting up private polyclinics under their own control. So, even in the Quebec structure, the physicians remain dominant, although seemingly not so much as in the provinces where opting out and extra billing were conceded by the provincial government from the beginning.

Why did the political forces in Quebec propose and eventually mandate a health services system that was so structured relative to the systems of other provinces and developed countries? Is the cultural homogeneity of the population of Quebec—with, as in Sweden, fewer "strangers"—a factor? Did the structural characteristics of the Catholic church carry over to health and welfare, to which the church contributed greatly until hospital care for the poor became too costly for a sectarian body to bear? The physicians purported to charge patients according to income limits, the so-called Robin Hood method, but this very traditional method was overridden by egalitarian values. To answer these questions would require a thorough knowledge of the social, cultural, and political history of the province.

In any case, logically structured as the Quebec plan seems, both Gosselin and Rodwin believe that the planning in Quebec failed relative to the objectives. In practice, it has been difficult to involve local constituencies at the planning level. Citizens have appeared only after a decision has been made to change existing patterns; local areas have been reluctant to fit into a regional pattern. In fact, some observers believe that the health care system may be heading toward inertia, stalemated on local decision making, the opposite of what the decentralization concept intended. Rodwin cited Castonguay himself as concluding pessimistically that, despite the hope that local committees would think in terms of prevention, education for health, rehabilitation, and general improvement in health levels of the population and that they would work as teams, their inclination and ability to do so were overestimated: no one really cared about the global objectives.[10] One objective of the Quebec government has been met, however—budget control. The hospitals have systematically received less money than they have requested, and the province has greater control over the total budget for hospitals than do other provinces.

Implementation of Medicare in Canada

It would seem, then, that from the early 1970s on there was a shakedown and testing period of the national health insurance system that had been quite ingeniously put together over time through protracted discussions that eventually led to accepted working relationships between the provinces and the federal government. The result was a politically agreeable, equitable system. The period of hospital insurance from 1958 to the 1967 enactment of the federal act for insuring physician services was one of steady expansion, increasing accessibility, and increasing expenditures. This last, however, was taken in its stride as part of the expected nature of things. Then came the 1970s, and Canada, like many other countries, began to experience inflation, reduced revenues, and increased expenditures for health services. Planning as envisioned by the aborted Saskatchewan plan was not in the political or the public purview, and the open-ended health insurance plan began to compete with other provincial and national priorities. The federal government was becoming restive with the seemingly infinite commitment it had made to the provinces to help finance mandated services. In 1976, the federal government announced a cut of 15 percent.

Beginning in 1977, it ceased participating by means of specified shared costs or conditional grants. It agreed to give some leeway to the provinces in terms of corporate income tax, enabling the provinces to collect internally more taxes.[11] The federal government also began providing block grants, which in 1977 made up about 25 percent of total program costs, to ease the pressure on the provincial treasuries. The block grants are contingent on the provinces' continuing the four principles. Also, and very important as a symbol of provincial autonomy, the provinces are not subject to federal audit. Further, the magnitude of the block grants is adjusted with increases in the GNP, thus tying federal expenditures for health insurance to the state of the economy rather than to the costs of health services programs. The federal government contributes approximately 50 percent of the expenditures of the provinces, varying by the economic levels of the provinces.

The leveling off of physician incomes, which are negotiated between physician representatives and the provinces, naturally resulted in physician incomes falling behind the rate of inflation. The provinces, like other areas, delayed negotiations while inflation was rising rapidly. The recourse of the physicians was to extra bill, as was their legal right in all provinces except Quebec. In 1982–83 the main health care policy crisis was the extent to which physicians in nine provinces were actually extra billing, thus eroding the objective of health insurance. Originally, the provinces probably believed that the extra billing right would be exercised at politically tolerable levels. It was estimated that physicians who extra billed at one time or another varied from .5 percent in Newfoundland and British Columbia to 52.8 percent in Nova Scotia. The value of extra billing as a percentage of Medicare plan payments for insured services varied from .02 percent in New Brunswick to 3.5 percent in Ontario and Nova Scotia and 4.8 percent in Alberta.[12]

The percentages do not seem large, but there was political and public fear that extra billing would become rampant. The Liberal government then in power in Ottawa was alarmed and enacted legislation to curb this trend. The physicians could continue to extra bill, but the additional payments had to be put into an escrow fund for three years, during which time a definite decision would be made as to how to handle the problem. Ontario proscribed extra billing. The federal government threatened to reduce its grants to provinces that permitted extra billing. The reaction of the medical profession in Ontario, through the Ontario Medical Association, was Canada's third physician strike. In Saskatchewan, it will be recalled, the provincial government gave in on the extra billing issue. In Ontario, however, the profession lost on the issue of extra billing, after a bitter, 25-day strike in June 1986. By 1986, the provinces had the power of the federal government behind them in the Canadian Health Act of 1984, which would penalize provinces that continued to permit extra billing.

Since 1986 Canada appears to have been in a holding pattern to contain the expansion of costs of its health insurance scheme. The two major, classic methods are limitations on supply—hospital beds and physicians—and budget capping instigated largely on the federal level. The federal government is attempting to push cost control to the provinces, which are "closer to the people," in the name of decentralization and to take the pressure off the federal government. The provinces, in turn, are finding that their desire for autonomy from federal interference has a painful spinoff in the form of more visible responsibility to the public and the providers.

Canada has learned that it cannot finance national health insurance through open-ended federal funding on a matching basis for the provinces. Such an arrangement provides provinces with little incentive to control expenditures. Thus, somewhat on the Swedish pattern, the sources of funding and responsibility for administration are close to the voters in the provinces, and provincial governments, rather than the federal government, become the major political targets. In recent years the expenditure level combining federal and provincial financing has been quite stable.

Summary

I place Canada to the right of Sweden in the market-minimized/market-maximized continuum because it retained intact the private, nonprofit ownership of the general hospitals and agreed to pay the privately practicing physicians on a fee-for-service basis. These accommodations left the health services delivery structure prior to universal health insurance relatively undisturbed except, of course, for the complete shift in funding from essentially private-sector sources to largely public sources—provincial and federal. At the same time Canada is more pluralistic in terms of decentralized sources of funding for capital and operating costs than the United Kingdom and Sweden but less so than the other countries in the continuum, which are still to be described.

Notes

1. Carl A. Meilicke and Janet L. Storch, "Introduction: An Historical Framework," in *Perspectives on Canadian Health and Social Services Policy: History and Emerging Trends,* ed. Carl A. Meilicke and Janet L. Storch (Ann Arbor, MI: Health Administration Press, 1980), pp. 3–18.

2. My major source is the magnificent study by Malcolm G. Taylor, *Health Insurance and Canadian Policy: The Seven Decisions that Created the Canadian Health Insurance System* (Montreal: McGill-Queens University Press, 1978). Other sources are: Spyros Andreopoulos, ed., *National Health Insurance: Can We Learn from Canada?* (New York: John Wiley & Sons, 1974), see particularly Chapter 1, "The Canadian Health Care System," by Maurice LeClair, pp. 11–96; and Gordon Hatcher, Peter R. Hatcher, and Eleanor C. Hatcher, "Health Services in Canada," in *Comparative Health Systems: Descriptive Analyses of Fourteen National Health Systems,* ed. Marshall W. Raffel (University Park, PA: Pennsylvania State University Press, 1984), pp. 86–132. In addition, I have experienced the Canadian political culture by being on the Faculty of Medicine, University of Western Ontario, London, Ontario from 1949 to 1952 with frequent visits to Canadian informants since then, most recently in 1984 and 1985. For the most recent source in extra billing, see Eric M. Meslin, "The Moral Costs of the Ontario Physicians' Strike," *Hastings Center Report* 17 (August–September 1987): 11–14.

3. Taylor, *Health Insurance and Canadian Policy.*

4. Malcolm G. Taylor, "The Canadian Health Insurance Program," in *Perspectives on Canadian Health,* ed. Meilicke and Storch, pp. 183–97. (Reprinted from *Public Administration Review* 33 (January–February 1973): 31–39.

5. Taylor, *Health Insurance and Canadian Policy,* p. 362.

6. The major sources for the Quebec story are: Malcolm G. Taylor, "Quebec Medicare: Policy Formulation in Conflict and Crises, in *"Health Insurance and Canadian Public Policy: The Seven Decisions that Created the Canadian Health System* (Montreal: McGill-Queens University Press, 1978), Chapter 7; Roger Gosselin, "Decentralization/Regionalization in Health Care: The Quebec Experience, *"Health Care Management Review* (Winter 1984): 7–25; Georges Desrosier, "Les Centres Locaux de Services Communitaires au Quebec I" and André-Pierre Contandriopoulos, "Economie du Systeme de Santé," in "Le Traite d'Anthropologie Medicale." (Unpublished papers prepared at the request of J. Dufresne of L'Institut Quebecois de Recherche sur La Culture, October 1983); François Champagne, André-Pierre Contandriopoulos, Marc-André Fournier, and Claudine Laurier, "Pursuit of Equity, Respect of Liberties and Control of Health Care Costs in Quebec," unpublished, n.d. (likely 1984); André-Pierre Contandriopoulos and Marc-André Fournier, "Les Services Medicaux au Quebec." (Unpublished paper prepared at the request of U. Reinhardt for the monograph "Physician Compensation under Fee for Service," Princeton University, June 1983.)

7. Taylor, *Health Insurance and Canadian Policy,* p. 402.

8. Ibid., p. 40.

9. Gosselin, "Decentralization/Regionalization in Health Care," pp. 7–25; Victor G. Rodwin, *The Health Planning Predicament: France, Quebec, England and the United States* (Berkeley: University of California Press, 1984).

10. Rodwin, *The Health Planning Predicament*, p. 130.
11. R. J. Van Loon, "From Shared Cost to Block Funding and Beyond: The Politics of Health Insurance in Canada," in *Perspectives on Canadian Health*, ed. Meilicke and Storch, pp. 342–66. Reprinted from *Journal of Health Politics, Policy and Law* 2 (Winter 1978): 454–78.
12. Pram Manga, *The Political Economy of Extra Billing* (Ottawa: Canadian Council on Social Development, 1983), p. 23.

Chapter 6

Western Europe

Because of a cluster of common characteristics, a number of countries can be placed in the same part of the market-minimized/market-maximized continuum. I have, rather arbitrarily, chosen West Germany (the Federal Republic of Germany) and France to represent countries in a middle range in the continuum, countries with a Continental European pattern of health services delivery systems and funding, and I place France relatively closer to the market-maximized end of the continuum. West Germany and France, along with Belgium, the Netherlands, and Switzerland, share basically similar characteristics while differing in styles of administration and negotiation between the private and public sectors. Portugal, Spain, and Italy have also been entering the league of industrialized and liberal-democratic nations; their health services delivery systems and financing are experiencing the same evolutionary development as the countries farther north, but in a much shorter span of time.

The common past of these countries lay in the feudal structure of the Middle Ages, with its division of labor among the artisans and the benefit associations and friendly societies or guilds of workers; the economic base and sources of funding for health services were established by the end of the nineteenth century. With varying degrees of paternalism and in keeping with a feudal tradition of responsibility for one's servants, governments and employers instituted social insurance and health insurance programs. All adults eventually gained the right to vote in democratic elections, and employees were able to organize through trade and industrial unions. Social insurance and health insurance became bargaining issues for labor and management within an administrative and political framework. In time, with the erosion of earlier customs, the master-servant relationship became a market bargaining model.[1]

Obviously, this is a bold and possibly cavalier synthesis of several centuries of European history, but even an impressionistic review reveals in the countries of Western Europe the familiar stages in the development of their health services delivery systems: (1) the establishment of an infrastructure of personnel and facilities; (2) development of the methods of finance—third party payers; and (3) the period of management and control. Jan Blanpain and others studied West Germany, England and Wales, France, the Netherlands, and Sweden and found that the health resources of all went through a similar sequence of stages, responded to similar problems, and were conditioned by the same matrix of forces and events produced by the industrial revolution and the later interest on the part of workers in making provisions for personal health services.[2] The descriptions of West Germany and France in the present work will highlight similarities and differences in health services, using proportions of sources of funding, charges at time of service, planning propensities, methods of reimbursement, and hospital ownership as measures.

West Germany

From Bismarck, 1881 to 1911

The Germany that unified under the leadership of Otto von Bismarck in the latter nineteenth century may be regarded as the most paternalistic parliamentary government on the European continent. The government feared growing socialism among the workers, who wished an increasingly larger portion of the economic surplus. The usual story has it that Bismarck "spiked the socialist guns" by making Germany in 1883 the first industrializing country to establish some form of compulsory health insurance for workers under certain incomes.

Insurance against loss of income because of sickness, or calling for some benefits for physician and hospital services, was by no means unknown in Germany even before Bismarck (e.g., in the coal and steel mines), so there were precedents. After Germany was unified, the concept of insurance became national in scope, but it was hardly universal. In 1885, only 10 percent of the population was covered by insurance, a figure that climbed to 22 percent by 1910.[3]

This early health insurance for workers covered physician services, drugs, spectacles, and hospital care. There was no charge at the time of service. The insurance was funded by payroll deductions from workers' wages and by proportional contributions from employers, at a ratio of two-thirds from workers and one-third from employers. This method of financing the day-to-day operation of health insurance became common everywhere in liberal-democratic and free-enterprise countries. Health insurance became a cost of production eventually paid for by higher prices on goods and services rather than through general revenue. The progressive personal income tax did not even exist at this time in the nineteenth century.

It was customary, given traditional worker affiliations, to administer the health insurance program through the existing mutual funds and benefit associations, which were very common. These funds in turn contracted with physicians and hospitals and were governed by representatives of employers and workers in proportion to their contributions. Funds set up by local governments were governed by locally elected representatives.[4] There was worker participation from the beginning.

Because of its early start, Germany is the only country that inaugurated compulsory health insurance without physician opposition, or even consultation. It is doubtful that most physicians even knew that Bismarck was considering health insurance. At the time, the medical profession was weak, unorganized, and not very well regarded; this was before the rapid advent of rational-reductionist, modern medicine based on the biological and chemical sciences.

As the years went by, however, physicians began to group together. Their growing professional self-consciousness was incorporating and monopolizing, through legal means, the expanding medical technical skills, particularly surgery. The public came to desire their skills, and medical care was already relatively expensive. After Germany had experienced health insurance for 27 years, the Englishman I. G. Gibbon, one of the earliest systematic observers of health insurance wrote of the endlessly problematic nature of personal health services and collective financing, "The meddlesome interference of lay control (through the governing boards) is one of the principal grievances of doctors against insurance societies."[5] In 1900 in Leipzig the physicians organized the Hartmannbund association of German physicians (named after Dr. Hermann Hartmann) to counter the power the sickness societies held over them. The issue of patients' freedom to seek care from physicians of their own choosing was, on the part of both physicians and patients, one of the most bitter causes of conflict with the administration of the sickness societies. Employers also opposed free choice, presumably because it was an inefficient method of providing physician services, and they were already complaining about the "abuse" (i.e., wasteful use) of hospital care. Gibbon reported, "One of the principal reasons given for the mischief is that, under present conditions, doctors often have no incentive to give troublesome and irksome treatment to a patient at his home."[6] He further observed that the very existence of hospital beds, the number of which had increased greatly between 1883 and 1910, automatically "increased use."[7] It is a truism that the demands for admission grow with the number of places available—shades of Roemer's law, which described the same phenomenon on the North American continent in the 1950s![8]

By the turn of the century in Germany, Gibbon observed that the medical profession had been brought into the full stream of economic forces. There were strikes of physicians against the sickness societies in Cologne and Leipzig. The societies in turn imported physicians from other parts of Germany to provide continuing services. There was also fear of hypochondriacs and malingering—all this as early as 1910. A final quotation from Gibbon is pertinent:

> The plea of the doctors is not wholly based on remuneration. Behind it lies to some extent the dignity of the profession. They fear that with low pay they will do scurried work, that they will become mere tongue and bottle drudges, treaters of symptoms hurrying through a round of medical routine instead of trained experts thoughtfully weighing delicate indications and applying remedies with skilled knowledge which will attack ailments at their sources.[9]

Even at that time there was a "cost explosion." It was not related to national budgets; rather, it was largely in the private sector of funding from employers and employees. In general, capitation payments to physicians doubled in all German sickness society funds regardless of type from 1888 to 1910.[10] Reasons given for the increases were better services (or, as economists would say today, a "little better product"), more specialized treatment, increases in remuneration to providers because of increased costs, and a rising standard of living. The cost of hospital construction per bed rose from 100 marks to 400 to 500 marks in a couple of decades after 1885. The number of physicians in 1885 in proportion to the population was roughly one to 3,000; by 1910, the proportion had been lowered to one in 2,000. Gibbon asserts that it is an undisputed fact that there was more demand for the services of physicians in 1910 than formerly. People were seeing physicians for slight ailments which "our ancestors would have allowed to run their course, to good or ill, without medical aid[11] We are still hearing this today.

The major policy and operating problems were found in the agreements between physicians and the sickness societies. Some amendments to the Act of 1883 authorized the sickness societies to limit the number of physicians accepted for practice for insured members and gave the societies the power to pick and choose physicians, despite the fact that physicians and patients wanted an open system of choice. The sickness societies were also given the power to establish a pooled fund to pay physicians, setting a limit on their remuneration regardless of the number of units of service rendered. These changes in the Act of 1883 resulted in individual contracts between physicians and the sickness societies. As the number of workers and dependents with insurance grew, so did the bargaining power of the societies, since the proportion of patients for private practice was eroded. The sickness societies used their bargaining power to keep payments to physicians relatively low. For almost 40 years the relationship between the societies and the medical profession was dominated by the issues of physician access to sickness society practice and patients and of patient freedom of choice.[12] During these years, culminating in 1931, increasingly detailed agreements were negotiated.

1911–1945

In 1911, the opposition of organized medicine through its new Hartmannbund polarized when the government enacted the National Health Insurance Act. This act considerably increased (or at least so the profession thought) the income limits for workers to be insured under the 1883 act, and it was also applied to servants and agricultural workers. Physicians realistically saw the 1911 act as a further erosion of their income levels and professional principles. Organized medicine insisted on freedom of choice for both physician and patient, fee-for-service payments, and a limited role for sickness societies. This last meant that the societies should not be in a position to influence unduly the organization and delivery of physician services.

The medical profession now appeared to consider itself to be well enough organized to prepare for a general strike to start January 1, 1914. The government attempted to reconcile organized medicine and the sickness societies, which were, in effect, the physicians' employers as delegated by the government. An agreement was reached December 23, 1913, only eight days before the strike deadline. Medical school faculty mediated the agreement, an indication of the prestige of academics in Germany, and it had a ten-year term.

The agreement included the following provisions: (1) the size of practice for sickness society physicians was set at one physician per 1,350 insured members, or one physician per 1,000 members when dependents were included; (2) a register was established for physicians to indicate their interest in being appointed to a sickness society panel; (3) appointments of physicians for insurance practice were to be made by a committee composed of medical and society representatives; (4) a contract committee, similarly composed, was to approve any individual contact between a physician and a sickness society; and (5) the government was to make arbitration services available. The issue of free choice, because of its volatility, was left open. This resulted in a wide range of local arrangements, perhaps a function of the strength and feelings of local physicians.

World War I (1914–18) upset the tenuous equilibrium, and the postwar inflation further strained the relationships between physicians and sickness societies, leading to new confrontations. In 1923, when the ten-year agreement ended, the government passed an emergency decree calling for an official arbitration machinery, setting standards for contracts, formulating rules for paying physicians, and protecting the sickness societies from "excessive" claims. The medical profession went on strike for three months. Eventually, in 1931, there was a new agreement, one that was regarded as a victory for the physicians. Preceding laws had favored the sickness societies by enabling them to direct the development of health insurance and health organization in Germany. But in 1931, the physicians gained recognition as a national bargaining power for the profession. Previously, the physicians had been dealt with individually. From 1931, then, the physicians for all practical purposes determined their own destiny, and the sickness societies served more like reimbursement than directing agencies.

The victory of the National Socialist Party (Nazis) in 1933 strengthened the position of the medical profession and diminished the influence of the sickness societies. National Socialism emphasized health as a national priority in order to build a strong army and work force. Blanpain suggests that the policy was health at any price, with the responsibility for attaining this objective placed on the medical profession.[13] All physicians had to join a central national body. Controls on volume of services did not fit with national health policy. Thus Germany at the end of World War II had, according to Blanpain, a well-organized medical establishment that had achieved a higher status in German society. This is not to say that the German medical profession was unique in that respect; the profession in all industrialized countries had achieved status and favor. The role played by National Socialism was, however, possibly quite peculiar to Germany. The machinery of the sickness society had almost completely deteriorated.

There were then over 1,500 societies classified into seven groups: (1) general local societies, (2) societies of the states (Länder), (3) factory societies, (4) trade association societies, (5) seamen's societies, (6) miners' societies, and (7) mutual benefit societies. These were split into local and national societies, the latter made up of seamen, miners, and mutual benefit societies. Their great number made it difficult for them to negotiate from unified strength with physicians, who were represented by their own stable organization.

1945–1985

After the war, the government made no attempts to change this uneven balance of power. Since 1960 the dominant issue has been how to control the physicians' fee structure.[14] Only in the 1950s did concern with hospital reimbursement become important, finally leading to the Hospital Finance Act of 1972. The same sequence was followed in many countries, with the hospital, among the various service components, becoming a major factor in costs, which increased faster than the gross national product and consumer price index. This engaged the government on another front of cost escalation, the hospitals being easier to take on politically than the physicians. There were the usual allegations of too many hospital beds and of wasteful utilization. Reducing the number of hospital beds, however, was politically explosive.

As early as 1954 Germany's minister of economic affairs used his authority in price control to set forth directives aimed at containing hospital reimbursement. The government simply limited the charges that hospitals could submit to the sickness funds. If these limits did not cover what the hospitals regarded as their costs, excess costs were to be covered by the hospital owners, public authorities, private sponsors, or as a last resort by hospital surpluses. In short, there was a budget cap, which had become a standard method of cost control everywhere. The states evolved a variety of patterns in dealing with hospital costs.

The Hospital Finance Act of 1972 regulated both the sickness societies' reimbursements to hospitals and the criteria of planning for hospital beds regionally. The government intended to use a grants-in-aid mechanism, familiar in the United States, to mitigate the widespread and unplanned growth of hospitals. As for reimbursements, the act aimed at keeping them within "socially acceptable limits," a phrase implying that there are no solid criteria but rather an equilibrium point between interests. The physicians in private practice, that is, outside the hospital, were not affected, as the hospital-based physicians were not well enough organized to act as a pressure group. Planning, the other focus of the 1972 act, has not been conspicuously successful, because of opposition against the closing of local and specialized hospitals of fewer than 100 beds and against the elimination of accommodations for private patients, which were regarded as an expensive luxury. The diversity of hospital ownership in Europe makes planning even more difficult politically. In West Germany in 1980 there were 3,230 hospitals and 707,800 beds. Of the hospitals, 37 percent were publicly owned (mainly by local governments), and they accounted for 52 percent of the beds. Thirty-four percent of the hospitals, with 35 percent of the beds, were nonprofit (many of them sectarian), and 29 percent of the hospitals with 13 percent of the beds were purely privately owned.[15] It will be recalled that sickness societies still contract directly with them under government regulations.

Siegfried Eichhorn observed that the network of sickness societies is the "cornerstone" of the West German health services system. Still, it would seem that the medical profession has been allotted not only tremendous power but also great responsibility.[16] The sickness societies may be the cornerstone, but the medical profession controlled the edifice during and after the stone was laid, and construction is still underway. The development of professional power and responsibility can be seen in the contemporary structure of relationships. The apparent intent of government policy was to put the bulk of the responsibility for physician services on the profession itself; over the decades it vociferously proposed certain principles: fee-for-service, free choice, and little or no financial or volume controls from the funding agencies. Hospital financing was out of the profession's jurisdiction.

Physicians in private practice who have sickness society patients must join an association of sickness society physicians—a Kassenarztliche Vereinigungen, or KV. There are also KVs on the federal level. The KVs set up joint commissions with sickness societies at both federal and state levels. The KVs are legally responsible for assuring that sickness society members have available to them around-the-clock ambulatory care, including emergency and standby services. The KVs must draw up long-term plans for staffing; they are responsible to the sickness funds and in turn are responsible to their members in guaranteeing that physicians meet obligations; the KVs represent the interests of contracting physicians with the societies. To what extent these legally set responsibilities are in fact carried out to the satisfaction of all concerned is not fully known. In any case, the KVs may not exclude any qualified physicians from sickness society practice. KVs may, however, cancel physicians' sickness society contracts for gross medical impropriety. Patients have free choice of physicians. There is no gatekeeper and therefore no panel. Since there is no panel, physicians are paid on a fee-for-service basis.

When the panel system was in effect, prior to the 1960s, physicians had to share a pooled fund and were therefore at risk. If their claims exceeded the pooled fund, each physician took a cut in payment. Since 1965 physicians have been paid fee-for-service based on their claims. Many physicians prefer this to the panel system of reimbursement, but the fee-for-service reimbursement arrangement requires that a long list of services be defined and reimbursed and that relative values between procedures be established, for example, the value of an appendectomy relative to a colonectomy. Before 1977 such values were negotiated on the state level, resulting in a wide range among states.

In 1977, a physician services cost containment law was passed, specifying a single list of definitions of service nationwide. The monetary value of each service, however, could still differ between societies and states. Although there is still no uniformity, there may be greater pressure for standardization of fees. Sickness societies still negotiate with KVs on the state level about total amount of money to be allocated to them. The societies, of course, have to stay within their incomes from employer and employee payroll deductions, which in 1977 became tied to the average wage and to the proportion deducted for insurance. These ties serve as external controls on physicians' incomes. If the fees claimed by the physicians exceed the income of the sickness societies, the KVs reduce the relative values of the fees per procedure and thus limit the total reimbursement to the physicians. Each year the KVs and sickness societies at the federal level must recommend the total budget deemed necessary. The physicians, then, are still somewhat at risk, and they are sure to exercise an internal utilization review of ambulatory services.

In no other country is there an arrangement whereby the government sets up an operating framework and rules and then leaves the physicians, through their own organizations and the insurance organizations, to operate the system with little direct government intervention. The arrangement raises some intriguing questions as to why Germany did not abolish the sickness societies, as did France in 1945 and Great Britain in 1946. Were the societies so entrenched in the German system that their existence was taken for granted?[17] Perhaps something in the body politic generates a seeming need for an "invisible hand" of social values and accommodations of interest groups, transcending the simple conceptual elegance of the invisible hand of the laissez faire market. Germany established a Concerted Action Conference.

In accordance with the law of 1977, Eichhorn calls the concept of the conference a notable innovation whose influence is difficult to evaluate.[18] The minister of labor and social affairs calls the conference twice a year. Its members are representatives of the association of sickness societies; the associations of physicians, dentists, and pharmacists; the associations of the pharmaceutical industry, hospitals, labor unions, and employers; and the states, municipalities, counties, and other government ministries. It has the stupendous charge to make recommendations (it is not a legislative body) about the total pool of funds for physicians and dentists and the total sums for prescriptions. Recommendations should also be made regarding "effectiveness, efficiency, and rationalization of the health system." In order to base these recommendations on facts, the conference is to make suggestions about gathering basic medical and economic information to help formulate policy. It is of interest that the parliament and the bureaucracy are inferentially not considered adequate for the purpose of the conference. Health care transcends the crass machinations of the political arena where it of course ends up anyway. It may be that a seeming consensus among interest groups will help the politicians decide what is politically feasible and administratively manageable.

Apparently the Concerted Action Conference is not so directly concerned with the hospitals as with the physicians and their financial relationship with the sickness funds. The federal government takes more direct action with respect to prices and the supply of hospitals than with respect to physicians. As suggested earlier, this began in 1954. Hospital deficits subsequently became an intense political issue. The 1972 law, briefly alluded to above, was intended to protect the financial position of hospitals and to regulate the per diem charges to the sickness societies. The law was based on the concept of cost reimbursement. The costs incurred by an individual hospital would be reimbursed fully as long as the hospital was regarded as operating effectively and economically. Costs are divided into operating and investment costs, with operating costs charged to the sickness societies and investment costs paid from federal, state, and local government taxes.

In 1973, the federal government broadened the law to include regulation of the pricing of daily operations. As for the supply of beds, federal, state, and local authorities cooperate on the financing of capital costs and are thus potentially able to control the supply. The 1973 law also enters into regional hospital planning and gives some statutory power to controlling supply. Each state draws up a hospital plan that estimates the number of hospital beds to be provided and allocates their distribution. The combined levels of government exercise financial control. In hospital planning, state government authorities confer with the state hospital association and parallel associations of sickness societies. Planning is primarily by consensus management. It is difficult to determine to what extent hospital planning in West Germany is negative planning, that is, stopping something from starting, or positive planning—directing where hospitals should be built and providing the money for them. Eichhorn observes that since 1972 government regulations on capital expenditures for hospitals have not yet shown any effect, for there are continuing and large differences in the distribution of hospital beds.[19] Even so, approximately 20,000 of roughly 700,000 hospital beds have been eliminated, less than 3 percent of the total. As in other countries, the closing of hospitals is a very controversial issue in local areas affected.

Summary

West Germany is quite clearly in the middle of the market-minimized/market-maximized continuum as compared with the countries already described. The country's health services delivery system has evolved from the historical roots of private sickness insurance societies, which were turned into agents of the government for administering the collection and payment of insurance monies to the physicians and hospitals. Also the government has placed a great deal of responsibility on the medical profession to manage its affairs so that there is relatively easy access to physician services and some control over health care expenditures. The health services financing and delivery structure is thus an interesting example of the intertwining of the public and private sectors, held together by a consensus as to how the federal government, the *Länder*, and the parties at interest should work together through corporate structures.

France

While Germany evolved a decentralized funding and administrative structure of sickness societies financed through employers and employee compulsory contributions, its immediate neighbor, France, established a centralized administrative system eventually abolishing the sickness societies and benefit associations. The historical reasons for this difference are hardly clear. Although regarded as a cradle of democracy after the bloody revolution of 1789, France established in Paris a new form of centralized authority, which is apparent in the operation of the French health services.[20] The government has to defer to and accommodate tensions among the major interest groups, yet, although France is divided into 95 administrative units called departments, ultimate power lies in Paris in the French Parliament and the president, and there lies the taxing power.

Jean-François Lacronique observes that the French health care system tries to conciliate two major ideological orientations that are inherently contradictory, at least according to the penchant for logic attributed to French rationalism.[21] One is egalitarianism as expressed in the French constitution; the second is liberalism, the individual freedom to pursue one's economic ambitions with little government regulation. The great majority of French physicians are private practitioners paid directly by fees from the patient. The patient then submits a claim to the government agency which in turn refunds the fee.

1930–1958

Governmental proposals to establish a health insurance plan began in France about 1930, by which time the health services infrastructure was firmly in place.[22] By this time, unlike Germany in 1883, the French medical profession was well organized, and it moved rapidly to head off government health insurance or at the very least to place itself in a position to protect its economic and professional interests. In 1927, the profession had adopted its well-known Medical Charter formulating four basic principles governing the relationship between physicians and health insurance funds: (1) the patient must be free to choose a physician; (2) the physician must be free to prescribe medications; (3) the physician and the patient must be allowed to bargain directly over the fee; and (4) professional privacy must be respected. These four principles were a response to previous proposals during the decade, which called for contractual agreements between health insurance funds and the physicians as a group and decreed a capitation method of payment. At this time capitation was the practice in Germany, one which, it will be recalled, was modified considerably after 1960.

In 1930, the French health insurance plan was part of an overall social security program using compulsory payroll deductions as the major source of funding. The 1930 act on social insurance distinguished between compulsory insurance and voluntary insurance. All workers in industry and commerce who were under 60 years of age and earning less than a certain income were mandated to be insured. Voluntary insurance was offered to farmers and others in agricultural pursuits and to small employers and white collar workers below a certain minimum income. Dependents under 16 years of age were also included.

Employers, employees, and some state subsidy financed the scheme, and there was some copayment to discourage trivial use. State subsidy varied according to the excess of costs over contributions. The state subsidy for farmers, for example, was relatively high. The benefits were the services of general practitioners and specialists, drugs, appliances, hospital care, surgery, and dental prostheses. In this early period of French health insurance the scheme was generally administered by the funds or societies developed in the nineteenth century by labor unions, employers' organizations, and parishes, the latter presumably sectarian. The insured could choose any health insurance fund. The French departments (i.e., state administrative units) set up public funds for those who had not made a selection. In accordance with the Medical Charter of 1927, the physicians did not have a fee schedule. The patients paid them directly and were to be reimbursed by the insurance funds, thus maintaining the traditional fiduciary relationship of physician and patient. This arrangement continued until 1945, when the multiple funds and societies were replaced by one official fund for each of the 95 departments. The objective presumably was to simplify the administrative organization by reducing the number of funding sources. The implementation of the law of 1945 was not regarded as particularly meaningful, for the government still did not achieve the degree of control that it wanted. In 1967 there was a major reform of the entire social security system, of which health insurance was an increasingly important part. Three national funds within the social security system were created, one of which was health insurance (Caisse Nationale d'Assurance Maladie des Travailleurs Salariés, or CNAMTS). The other two were for invalidity and industrial accidents and for pensions. Each fund was given some autonomy to balance income and outgo. The local and regional funds were placed under the supervision of the national system. The governance of the national funds was joined by representatives of the trade unions and of the employers (Confédération Nationale du Patronat Français, or CNPF).

Victor Rodwin, an excellent observer of the French scene, claims that with the French trade unions ideologically divided and the CNPF united, the government and the CNPF actually shared power.[23] With the law of 1967, the CNAMTS became the dominant source of funds for health services. This established a countervailing power that reduced the diffused pluralism of the previous funding sources, which was what the physicians' negotiating organizations feared, that is, one source of funding. According to Rodwin, the CNAMTS had agreed not to compete with the private practice of physicians by establishing its own health centers for primary care. Rather, all physicians would participate in the health insurance scheme. In 1971 the CNAMTS began to consider ways of monitoring the practice and prescribing patterns of physicians.

1958–1986

France, like other countries, eventually found another problem when political emphasis shifted from physicians to hospitals: hospital costs were outstripping all economic indicators. The 1958 Hospital Reform Act during Charles De Gaulle's presidency had merged university medical schools with the best-equipped public hospitals and created many medical-academic professorial positions. Public hospitals became open to all, which enhanced both their prestige and their ability to attract highly qualified clinicians. High-ranking clinical professors resented the goal of creating full-time salaried clinicians in the public hospitals because they wished to preserve that portion of private practice that permitted them to treat their private patients in private beds in the public hospitals.

Public hospitals in France have not been highly regarded by the public in comparison with private hospitals. Seventy percent of the hospitals are private, but the public hospitals have most of the beds—about 70 percent. Most of the private hospitals are called *cliniques* and are proprietary. In the middle 1970s, planners in the ministry of health improved and expanded the capacity of the French public hospitals. Rodwin observed that the process revealed three problems: (1) conflicts between public hospitals and *cliniques*, (2) uneven distribution of beds, and (3) a rapid increase in expenditures for hospitals.[24] It is unlikely the planners anticipated these problems.

Public hospitals lost patients to the *cliniques* because the *cliniques* were newer and brighter than the public hospitals. Since they did not have the public hospitals' concentration of high technology, the *cliniques* asserted they were less expensive than public hospitals and hence more efficient. The *cliniques* were accused of caring for patients who were not as sick and who therefore required less expensive treatments. The number of private hospital beds increased faster than the number of public beds, and private hospitals had easier access to capital.

The 1979 amendments to the hospital law gave the minister of health discretionary power to eliminate hospital beds that were classified as unnecessary—those with an occupancy rate of less than 40 percent. About 7,000 hospital beds out of roughly 587,000 (approximately 1 percent) were scheduled to be eliminated. There was furious criticism from both the majority party and the opposition, and the cuts were never made.[25]

In May 1981, the first Socialist president, François Mitterand, was elected, and the dissolution of the National Assembly followed. The Socialists held a majority of the new chamber, the Senate majority was still Conservative, and the new minister of health was a member of the French Communist party. It was then expected that there would be an unprecedented series of reforms. But the new government, according to Jean-François Lacronique, seemed to move slowly. In mid-1982 the government made public a Plan for Health (Charte de la Santé) which stated that private institutions are an integral part of the French system. Mitterand, in his election campaign, had promised to eliminate the private sector in public hospitals, that is, to do away with clinical professors' being able to treat their private patients in them. Heated negotiations in the fall of 1981 between the medical profession and the government resulted in the creation of an association of physicians called Medical Solidarity (Solidarité Médical). In June 1982 (though not to be effective until January 1986), the government moved to withdraw clinicians' privilege of treating private patients in public hospitals; in return, the physicians would receive increased social insurance benefits and a more generous pension. Lacronique remarked that "a subtle balance between public and private initiative has so far been preserved in almost all types of service and does not seem to be doomed by the new Socialist government, although the health sector was placed under the responsibility of a Communist minister."[26]

This situation seems to illustrate that, in politics, full responsibility creates caution; this may be especially true in a liberal-democratic country where the previous office-holders can be regarded as the loyal opposition. In such a political context, neither capitalism and laissez faire nor socialist-egalitarianism and economic planning can operate in their pure forms. The extremely pluralistic nature of the French political and economic system would seem to be so historically rooted that socialism in its orthodox form cannot be applied to any meaningful extent, even in the health services. Interest groups are so vociferous and respected that the narrow consensus required in a socialist state cannot be achieved.

As a final illustration of the extreme dynamism of French health care policy, let me add that by late 1988, the time of this writing, France had gained a Conservative government, and the Communist minister of health had resigned, apparently because the Socialist government was supporting the French medical status quo.

Summary

I place France, along with West Germany, in the middle of the market-minimized/market-maximized continuum because of its comparatively pluralistic nature, despite the apparent central control that the government exercises over the public sector. The country has a national health insurance system in principle, but even by American standards, the French health care delivery system is very pluralistic. The pluralism is expressed in the freedom of the private sector to function and expand outside of the public sector. The French are allowed amenity options through the private *cliniques,* and the public hospitals are the major backup for high technology medicine. The French health services delivery and financing system then appears relatively loose and unstructured. Conventional wisdom would have it that this is congenial to the French national character.

Notes

1. William McNeil, *The Rise of the West: A History of the Human Community* (Chicago: University of Chicago Press, 1963). See particularly the section on the feudal system.
2. Jan Blanpain, with Luc Delesie and Herman Nys, *National Health Insurance and Health Resources: The European Experience* (Cambridge, MA: Harvard University Press, 1978), p. 209.
3. I. G. Gibbon, *Medical Benefit: A Study of the Experience of Germany and Denmark* (London: King, 1912), p. 2.
4. Blanpain, *National Health Insurance,* p. 25.
5. Gibbon, *Medical Benefit,* p. 22.
6. Ibid., p. 89.
7. Ibid., p. 198.
8. Milton I. Roemer and Max Shain, "Hospital Utilization under Insurance," Hospital Monograph Series, No. 6 (Chicago: American Hospital Association, 1959).
9. Gibbon, *Medical Benefit,* p. 89.
10. Ibid., p. 67.
11. Ibid., p. 234.
12. Blanpain, *National Health Insurance,* p. 27. It appears that Blanpain et al. has the best historical summary of the German health services so far written; other sources drawn on for background, although not necessarily cited, are: Josef van Langendonck, *Prelude to Harmony on a Community Theme: The Health Care Insurance Policies in the Six and Britain* (London: Oxford University Press, 1975). Langendonck's book was inspired by the creation of the European Economic Community to analyze the implications for the health services delivery

systems in those cooperating countries and differences in health insurance benefits and source of funding. It is an outstanding book for the purpose of showing
how the difference in benefit ranges, methods of paying providers, and methods
of financing could complicate economic cooperation and the free flow of labor
between countries. There are, of course, gross similarities in patterns, but the
book does reveal the seemingly quixotic nature of these differences as products
of historical circumstances and incremental compromises. See also William A.
Glaser, *Health Insurance Bargaining: Foreign Lessons for Americans* (New York:
Gardner Press, 1978) and Glaser's *Paying the Doctor: Systems of Remuneration
and their Effects* (Baltimore, MD: Johns Hopkins University Press, 1970).

13. Blanpain, *National Health Insurance*, p. 30.
14. See Deborah Stone, *The Limits of Professional Power: National Health Care in
    the Federal Republic of Germany* (Chicago: University of Chicago Press, 1980)
    for more recent attempts to control physicians' fees.
15. Siegfried Eichhorn, "Health Services in the Federal Republic of Germany," in
    *Comparative Health Systems: Descriptive Analyses of Fourteen National Health
    Systems*, ed. Marshall W. Raffel (University Park, PA: Pennsylvania University
    Press, 1984), p. 327. This source is the most up-to-date description of the anat-
    omy of the West German health services, following Blanpain whose account
    ends around 1977.
16. Ibid., p. 310.
17. William A. Glaser, *Health Insurance Bargaining: Foreign Lessons for Americans*
    (New York: Gardner Press, 1978), p. 109; and Donald W. Light and Alexander
    Schuller, eds., *Political Values and Health Care: The German Experience*
    (Cambridge, MA: MIT Press, 1986).
18. Eichhorn, "Health Services in the Federal Republic of Germany," p. 303.
19. Ibid., p. 310.
20. Jean-François Lacronique, "Health Services in France," in *Comparative Health
    Systems: Descriptive Analyses of Fourteen National Health Systems*, ed. Mar-
    shall W. Raffel (University Park, PA: Pennsylvania State University Press, 1984),
    p. 258. This article is the most recent source for the French health services.
21. Ibid.
22. Blanpain, *National Health Insurance*, p. 100. This source is the most helpful one
    on the history of French health insurance.
23. Victor G. Rodwin, *The Health Planning Predicament: France, Quebec, England,
    and the United States* (Berkeley: University of California Press, 1984), p. 88.
24. Ibid., p. 93.
25. Lacronique, "Health Services in France," p. 273.
26. Ibid., p. 279.

Chapter 7

Australia

Before 1949

The development of the Australian health services delivery and financing system has borne a remarkable resemblance to the development of the U.S. system. Australia did not become a national entity until 1901. From the early nineteenth century until that time, the Australian subcontinent had evolved into six separate self-governing units, as immigrants, largely from the United Kingdom, came in increasing numbers. It is well known that the early immigrants were convicts and political dissenters shipped far enough away not to cause any more trouble in the home country. The self-governing units became Australia's six states, and their early isolation from one other as well as from the home country resulted in distinct state identities and an extreme distrust of central authority such as that represented by a federal government. This position was somewhat analogous to that of the thirteen colonies in the United States just after they united as a nation.

The nature of the Australian state-federal relationship profoundly affected the evolution of a national policy regarding the organization, ownership, and financing of personal health services, again analogous to the United States and to Canada. The states were accorded the power and responsibility for the health and welfare of their residents; the federal government was not to be involved. The Constitution of 1901 conceived of government as limited, according to the classical liberal-democratic theory of government. The country was opened to commercial development along the private enterprise lines of investment and entrepreneurship, a philosophy inherited from the parent country but carried out with an aggressiveness unhampered by the traditions of a monarchical and feudal past. Australia, like the United States, actually practiced the major tenets of the laissez faire philosophy, sharing the belief that personal health services were a personal affair, but that sanitary, environmental, and communicable disease control were public responsibilities lodged with the states.

According to Sax, Australia did not inherit the English framework of medical social organization, with its emphasis on residence as a prerequisite to obtaining services.[1] Sax also observes that it should not be surprising that those who valued independence, economic and political, as much as the early settlers—convicts included—were influenced by the new social morality of self-help, a philosophy propounded by religious nonconformist groups "who urged Christians to be enterprising, thrifty and hard-working." The analogy to New England's Puritans is very close. The first medical practitioners in Australia were employees of the Crown and ministered to prisoners and Crown employees. The rest of the population had to look after itself. What emerged in the atmosphere of self-help were systems of private medical care, free-care public hospitals, and contract medical practice through friendly societies or benefit associations. (These associations were numerous in England and were emulated in Australia.) According to Sax, these arrangements "were perceived as adequate in a society where individuals respond to their own needs in accordance with their means."[2]

In Australia it became customary for public-spirited citizens to donate money and form committees or corporations to establish nonprofit hospitals. They became known as voluntary hospitals as in the United States, Canada, and England. In Australia they also became known as public hospitals if they received subsidies from the state government. As the population began to evolve into a class structure toward the end of the nineteenth century, purely private hospitals emerged to serve those who did not wish to be in publicly subsidized, private, charity hospitals or could not be admitted as charity patients because they were too affluent. Physicians with hospital admission privileges donated their services in public hospitals and charged fees to private patients. In private hospitals presumably all patients were charged fees. As in the United States and Canada, physicians were freestanding practitioners with their own offices or with hospital staff privileges. There is no particular organizational logic to the North American and Australian pattern of freestanding physicians with hospital admission privileges or to the British and Continental pattern of hospital-based specialists and community-based general practitioners without hospital affiliations; these two patterns emerged as accommodations to circumstances related to the ability of physicians to earn a living mainly on fees from private patients. Also, the specialists and general practitioners were not distinct entities. In the new countries there was no history of structure like that of the royal speciality societies. There was less differentiation among physicians, and, as the new countries developed, differentiation appeared but not that of inpatient and outpatient practice sites.

Between the two World Wars, from 1918 to 1940, the public hospital became the most desired place in Australia for treatment of serious medical conditions because it was more likely to have special equipment and trained specialists than a private hospital. As the population grew and differentiated and the general hospital became a desirable place to be diagnosed and treated, there was, according to Sax, increasing demand among people who were not recognized as "proper" subjects for charity. They could not, however, be ignored either, because care in the relatively few, better-equipped, private hospitals was too expensive except for the very well-off. Quoting Thame,[3] Sax wrote that "means tests came to annoy those whom they excluded rather than to stigmatize those whom they admitted to care."[4]

In the natural course of events, and in accordance with the prevailing political philosophy in Australia, public hospitals had wards for the poor and other accommodations for those who could not pay for care. Australia's emerging middle classes felt that government should make available only those community services and goods that could not be provided by private enterprise.[5] This view became apparent in subsequent health services and political debates; it is analogous to the view familiar in the United States, that is, that provision of social benefits by government would erode self-reliance and mutual help by private means and encourage pauperism. Nevertheless, collective action through government came about in Australia as inevitably and incrementally as had been true in the history of welfare and social insurance in other liberal-democratic countries.

Collective actions evolving toward some kind of health insurance began as early as the 1920s, not because the working class was socialistic, but because the electorate became better informed. In 1923 there was a Royal Commission on Health Insurance. In 1928 a national health insurance bill was proposed, but the private friendly societies and the employers opposed it and it lacked electoral support. The Australian Medical Association (then called the British Medical Association and an affiliate) supported an indemnity scheme for the middle-income group and, presumably, charity for those with low income. Another bill was proposed in 1928 that was restricted to general practitioner services, emulating the British health insurance model of 1911. Clearly, the Australian personal health services had passed through the stage of the development of the infrastructure by 1930 and then entered the stage of third-party payment. A Labour government was in power from 1941 to 1949 and during the difficult World War II years. This government had proposals for health insurance free to all citizens regardless of income level. The Australian Medical Association refused even to enter into the debate, analogous to the position of the American Medical Association during the same period in the United States. National health insurance for Australia got as far as the Pharmaceutical Benefits Act of 1944. The Australian Medical Association declined to cooperate with the Act and pledged not to use the proposed formulary and prescription forms. The Australian judiciary declared it unconstitutional for the commonwealth to exercise the power of the act over physicians and pharmacists: to do so would be a form of conscription. In 1947, Parliament passed a second Pharmaceutical Act. The Australian Medical Association sued the commonwealth; again, the judiciary ruled in favor of the medical profession. Consequently, Australian physicians and dentists now bask under this protection against commonwealth regulation. Physicians cannot be compelled to accept salaried employment with the commonwealth, and they cannot be required by the commonwealth to provide services for a prescribed fee. Presumably, the states have the right of requirement, but under the circumstances it would not be feasible to exercise it. Nor can a physician in the United States be compelled to enter a salaried service or to accept a fee given by the federal government. The federal government might set up such salaried services and fixed fees, but physicians could elect to serve or not as they wished and could accept or reject prescribed fees, as for Medicaid and Medicare, by not entering into contracts with the federal government or, for that matter, with the states.

In 1945, the Hospital Benefits Act authorized the negotiation of agreements with the states for hospital benefits partially subsidized by the commonwealth. Participating states had to guarantee that accommodations, diagnosis, and treatment would be made available in the public wards of public hospitals free of charge, without a means test. The Tuberculosis Act of 1948 followed. The new Hospital Act started in 1946 with protests from the Australian Medical Association about the abolition of the means test. Physicians anticipated that they would have to provide care free of charge in public wards to patients who could not pay, but there was no change in previous custom. The scheme received no support in any state except Queensland after the defeat of the Labour government in 1949. It is apparent that there was no broad political support to maintain the act.

In 1948, the Labour government had proposed a far-reaching National Services Act. The Australian Medical Association refused even to nominate representatives to discuss the proposition. The act passed in November 1948, but its implementation was delayed because of the Australian Constitution with its division of powers between the commonwealth and the states and the electorate's fear of "socialism."

With the defeat of the Labour government in 1949, Australia embarked on a 20-year period under the Liberal-Agrarian party, which laid the groundwork for the very pluralistic health services delivery system and sources of funding that have continued in some form to this day. The Labour Government had set in motion collective action that had to be taken up in some form by the Liberal-Agrarian Party as its political response. In the Australian context, the term "liberal" means a political and economic philosophy based on the classical liberalism of nineteenth-century Britain, that is, limited government intervention in the economy and so far as possible limited provision by government of health and welfare services except for the poor. American liberals, on the other hand, modified this political tradition considerably beginning with the New Deal during the Depression of the 1930s. In Australia, the farm constituency joined forces with the business and industry constituency of the Liberal party.

1949–1972

The political response of the Liberal-Agrarian government to the momentum created by the defeated Labour party government during the 20 years from 1950 to 1970 was a marvel of political pragmatism that exceeded even the American genius for political compromise. The Liberal-Agrarian government produced a mixture of public hospitals and voluntary insurance, a program for the elderly, and public assistance for the poor. Left out were the self-employed, low-income workers, and farmers. The program had no compulsory enrollment, but voluntary insurance was subsidized to lower premiums and encourage enrollment. In addition to a program for those over age 70, the new government put into effect the Pharmaceutical Benefits Act of the previous Labour government, which had not actually been abandoned. Thus Australia began universal health insurance through pharmaceutical benefits plus special attention to the elderly.

Observers credit the Australian Medical Association with tremendous political power, as is also the case with the American Medical Association in the United States. But it seems that in Australia there was an effective alliance between the incumbent government and the medical association that is not seen to the same extent in the United States. In any case, the health services policies and programs of the Liberal-Agrarian government were congenial to the views of the Australian Medical Association in that the physicians continued to be paid a fee-for-service, public subsidies encouraged voluntary health insurance and reduced hospital costs, a portion of the expenses for physician services was reimbursed, and the physicians would accept payment directly from the government for services rendered to elderly patients.

This pluralistic pattern lasted until the early 1970s when the Labour party came back into power. Before then, however, there was growing discussion, debate, and criticism across party lines about the increasingly felt inequities of the Australian situation. Even the Liberals became concerned with the open-ended nature of the fees for physicians. Although the health insurance arrangements covered the majority of the population, many were left out: the poor with the stigma of the means test, the self-employed, and those in underserved areas. These were the familiar criticisms of the private and voluntary methods to achieve equity in Canada, the United States, Great Britain, and Sweden, as well as other countries in the liberal-democratic tradition. Government accounted for nearly 50 percent of total expenditures for health services for voluntary health insurance, physician fees, and hospital costs. Those who argued for universal health insurance said that government was already heavily involved.

In April 1968, toward the end of the Liberal-Agrarian government, Labour party opposition forced the appointment of a Senate select committee to examine the costs of hospital and physician services. The result was the Commonwealth Committee of Enquiry into Health Insurance, known as the Nimmo Committee. Its terms of reference were limited to voluntary health insurance, as to the extent of enrollment of the population and its costs. Two economists, R. B. Scotton and J. Deeble, presented their proposals for a universal health insurance plan that had already been presented to the Senate select committee.[6] It is of political interest that their proposals did not intend that all services had to be free to users, that all health services had to be centralized or nationalized, that physicians and hospitals had to be paid by any particular methods, that private insurance and methods were to be prescribed, or that there would be restrictions on the choice of physician. The proposals emphasized universal entitlement to specified services paid for by a single health services fund and administered by a commission created by statute and not delegated to private administrative agencies by contract. Sources of revenue were to come from a 1.25 percent levy on personal incomes, a matching Commonwealth subsidy, and deductions from wages and automobile insurance companies.

Under the goading, in large part, of the Labour opposition, the incumbent government following the Nimmo Committee recommendations had by 1970 worked out a more equitable arrangement for health services delivery than the political marble cake described earlier. Physician fees, however, continued to be a thorny issue both politically and administratively, given that the courts interpreted the Constitution as forbidding the commonwealth to mandate fees or methods of reimbursement. The federal government restructured the voluntary character of Australian health insurance by pouring large amounts of money into the system, but gaps remained. There were insufficient insurance funds to cover private hospital charges and insufficient benefits to cover charges for outpatient services in public hospitals. Psychiatric patients remained ineligible for insurance. So in July 1970, an improved "pluralism," a direct result of the Australian interest-group political process, set a precedent, according to some critics, that the Labour government repeated as the decade wore on.[7] "Members of the public, the registered funds [insurance companies], their agents, and many doctors bumbled along without clear guidance." "Bumbling along" is another term for incrementalism.

1972–1986

The Labour government which returned to office between 1972 and 1975 used its power to shift resources into the public sector, such redistribution being intended to achieve egalitarian objectives. Universal health insurance was a natural vehicle for reform in that framework. The previous Liberal-Agrarian coalition had provided public support only to specified groups—pensioners and veterans—with others encouraged to provide for themselves with help from public subsidies of the prevailing, more or less private, system. Even before the Labour party came into power late in 1972, it pushed for organizational changes in the health services delivery system, putting forth proposals to rationalize and integrate health services on a regional basis through the development of community-oriented health centers. Soon after the new government took office, it announced the establishment of a Hospitals and Health Services Commission, to expedite the community health services concept, which, of course, embodied basically a planning concept. The health centers would in time contain what was regarded as a key element in an integrated system—primary care as an entry point in the system. Structure is difficult to impose on a pluralistic system, in Australia just as in the United States, but the various states made beginnings. For the purpose of this book, however, it would seem that the health insurance and funding concept embodied in legislation known as Medibank I (because others followed) is of more pertinence, because it was backed by compulsion, an exceedingly controversial concept in Australia as in the United States. On this issue, however, even under a Labour government, compulsion was not met head on, but absorbed in a general universality described here.

Under Medibank I, the Labour government intended to eliminate, in large part, the financial barrier to health services, to share the burden of finances more equitably, to make administration more efficient, and presumably to make hidden subsidies more visible. Medibank I would replace the patchwork benefits of the previous administration's National Health Act with a single health insurance fund to finance physician and hospital services. A Health Insurance Commission with statutory powers for direct accountability to the government was to administer the program.

Physician services were to be paid up to 85 percent of the government-set schedule of fees, although physicians were not under contract to accept this fee schedule. The maximum difference between the fee and the benefit for any single procedure would be $5 (Australian). The method of reimbursement preferred by the government was for physicians to send claims to Medibank, periodically in bulk, and accept reimbursement as full payment. Physicians had, however, the option of billing patients directly. Inpatient care in public hospitals in ward-level accommodations, including services provided by hospital staff physicians, was to be provided free of charge and without a means test as were outpatient services at public hospitals. Hospital agreements would be negotiated with the states, and the commission would provide a subsidy of about 50 percent. Physicians providing care to patients in wards were to be paid by salaries and sessional payments (payments per hour or half day). Private rooms were available to private patients desiring them, and patients selecting private rooms could also have a free choice of hospital-based physicians at an extra charge. No such choice was granted for patients selecting ward accommodations. The health insurance fund was to be financed by a 1.35 percent levy on taxable incomes, a matching subsidy from the commonwealth, plus a levy on worker compensation and automobile insurance companies.

Low-income families were exempted from the income tax levy, and a ceiling was placed on levies on high-income taxpayers. It is of interest that even under a Labour government tax deductions or contributions to private health insurance companies would be continued. Some groups would have liked to proscribe even the existence of private health insurance, but the prevailing Australian political philosophy did not support such a notion, nor is it found anywhere among the liberal-democracies.

It took until November 1973 to bring the Health Insurance Commission Bill and the establishment of the commission to the floor of the House of Representatives. They were passed by the lower house but were rejected by the Senate, which was controlled by the Liberal-Agrarians. Sax observes that insurance companies and the private hospitals were decisive in this rejection.[8] The parliamentary procedure was repeated in April, 1974, with the same result. In apparent desperation the Labour prime minister dissolved the Parliament and called for a general election in May, hoping to get control of the Senate. Labour was returned to office but still did not control the Senate. During the election campaign, the Liberal-Agrarian coalition proposed an alternative health insurance scheme retaining the voluntary principle but not requiring the poor to pay for the insurance. Government would pay premiums, scaled by income level, to the health insurance fund on behalf of the poor.

In July 1974, Labour introduced its original health insurance proposals for the third time. The House accepted and the Senate rejected for the third time. In August 1974, the prime minister exercised for the first and only time in Australian history his constitutional power to convene the two houses simultaneously. The resulting passage of the bills presumably depended on the Labour majority in the House overriding the Liberal-Agrarian majority in the Senate. Through a legislative technicality, the Liberal-Agrarian opposition, however, forced the government to finance its health insurance proposal from general revenue and not from a personal income tax.

Medibank I went into effect in July 1975 with many obstacles of implementation to overcome, such as agreements with the states for hospital care and constant bickering between the Australian Medical Association and the government over fees and claims procedures. The private health insurance funds could negotiate to be administrators, but none came forward. Many believed that the private health insurance funds would fold, but they maintained their markets through advertising as alternatives to the government plan and developed "gap" insurance to cover extra charges for private rooms in hospitals, for choice of physicians, and for services not insured by Medibank I.

Medibank I was short-lived, caught up in larger political issues. The Conservative coalition returned to power at the end of 1975, only six months after Medibank I was put into effect. The election campaign issues were inflation and high taxes, which were to be managed by reducing government deficits and expenditures. Health care was obviously a target, because by this time it accounted for an increasing share of the gross domestic product, up from 5 percent in 1963–64 to 7.7 percent in 1975–76. Also, health care expenditures were taking a large share of direct government expenditures, pushing out other fiscal priorities. The new government promised not to dismantle Medibank, a popular program possibly transcending political lines in the body politic, and in January 1976 set up a committee of inquiry.

The primary objective of the new government was to reduce the pressure on the commonwealth budget by encouraging people to leave government health insurance in favor of private health insurance. By May 1976, the government had devised Medibank II, to go into effect in October 1976. The provisions of the proposal can be summarized as: (1) a health insurance levy of 2.5 percent on the personal income of those who worked and opted for coverage by Medibank; (2) those selecting Medibank would be entitled to physician services scaled to 85 percent of the fee schedule set by the government up to a maximum gap between the fee and the benefit of $5 (Australian); accommodations in public hospitals would be free as would treatment by physicians on the hospital staff; (3) those who chose Medibank and wished to be treated in the hospital by physicians of their choice would be required to buy private hospital accommodation insurance, but the physician fees would still be covered by public health insurance funds; (4) insurance contributions would no longer be deductible from personal income tax; and (5) additional insurance could be purchased by those wishing to cover charges for single rooms in public or private hospitals. It should be noted that Medibank II was still essentially compulsory in that all people needed to select one of three options: basic Medibank coverage in which there would be no charges, liberalized Medibank coverage for choice of physician in the hospital at an extra levy by the government, and purely private coverage outside of Medibank altogether. The government hoped that a large proportion of the public would buy private insurance and thus decrease the pressure on the commonwealth budget. I was told when I was in Australia in October 1976, shortly after the program went into effect, that the public sector of Medibank might act as a brake on total costs, including those of the private sector, because, if private insurance premiums rose unduly, people in private insurance could choose one of the two options in Medibank.[9]

During October, people needed to select their options, and there was great excitement as to what proportions of the population would select what options. Even through the proposal of the new government seemed complicated for the general public to understand fully, I was impressed by the clarity, simplicity, and copiousness of the information the government provided through television advertisements and pamphlets. After the smoke had cleared, 59 percent of the people had selected full private insurance, and another 10 percent had selected the supplementary "hospital-only" insurance, assuring free choice of physician while in the hospital. Thus, only 31 percent selected the basic Medibank II option.[10] Clearly, by this criterion Australia is a middle-class, relatively conservative country as far as using government in daily life is concerned. It seems, moreover, that the government succeeded in its objective of pushing more expenditures for health services to the private sector. Further, the national health planning agency, as such, was abolished. The states, however, could do whatever they wished with planning so long as they did not use commonwealth funds.

Expenditures for health services continued to increase, although at a slower pace, and the government was not yet satisfied with the results. The many interest groups were restive; no consensus on health services policy in a manageable form seemed to be forthcoming. The Conservative government thrashed around for solutions and solutions were not possible, given the inability of the country to pull together to achieve objectives. The main objective—to reduce the federal budget—could be achieved only at the cost of reducing the tenuous equity already present or paying no attention at all to the delivery system structure itself to get a handle on physician fees.

So, at a rather dizzying pace, and with a confusion of issues and elements, the government began to examine the details in Medibank II:

federal hospital subsidy, bulk billing (or not) by physicians, federal-state fiscal relationships, monitoring of physicians' practice patterns, the role of charges at time of service. The government went through two more Medibanks—III in May 1978 and IV in November 1978. Medibank IV made a change in substance with unknown consequences. The private insurance option was no longer compulsory! But nevertheless, in May 1979, Medibank V emerged, largely as a result of criticisms of the previous Medibank, and still the objective of the government was to reduce public expenditures. It was estimated that 15 percent of the insured persons dropped their insurance and became public patients when they were seriously ill. Private insurance enrollment was falling.

In 1979 the government created the Commission of Inquiry into the Efficiency and Administration of Hospitals, reporting in 1981, known as the Jamison Commission.[11] The chairman was a high ranking official in a large accounting firm, an appointment that obviously signified a fiscal emphasis. The commission had no easy task. It dealt with cost, resource allocation, efficiency, and cost control in hospitals and related facilities. The main concern, however, was the respective roles and responsibilities of the state and commonwealth governments. The commission was confronted with the political reality that the commonwealth government was not likely to give up its dominant financial position of control of the health services economy, given its overall fiscal responsibility for the country. The commission recommended (briefly paraphrased) that: (1) the commonwealth should set its objectives clearly so that the states knew what to expect; (2) in turn, the states should set their own objectives; (3) the cost-sharing objectives should be replaced by a commonwealth block grant to each state for health services that combined the present categorical grants (reminiscent of the United States); and (4) the grants should be contingent on the states' meeting specific conditions about the supply of beds, access to public hospitals for all patients, free care for pensioners, and special attention to the poor. Finally, but probably most significant, the commission recommended the establishment of a working party to formulate a new health insurance scheme.

The commission, not surprisingly, accepted the general political philosophy of the Conservative government and, possibly, indeed, of the body politic, by expanding the framework in which health insurance would be formulated and operated. It decided that the maintenance of a mixed economy in health services delivery is desirable, with private sector facilities, subsidized or not, coexisting with government-subsidized facilities.[12] The commission encouraged as many people as possible to provide for their physician and hospital care while retaining the voluntary character of insurance arrangements.[13] While recognizing the possibility of duplication of hospital-based high technology, the commission observed that "a hospital which sincerely believes it needs a particular super-speciality for it to perform the role it sees for itself is not very receptive to rhetoric of rationalizers, and can usually produce arguments against which the only recourse may be arbitrary edict—which authorities are reluctant to use."[14] The emphasis should be on voluntary cooperation and self-regulation rather than on the "rigid imposition of mandatory procedures." A flash of insight, the implications of which were not elaborated, was expressed: "There are no internationally accepted guidelines for the priorities of services."[15] In other words, and to repeat, in a liberal-democratic political system health services policy and implementation are a negotiated system trying to achieve a balance between interest groups.

Medibank VI became effective in September 1981, and it reflected a return to the basic principles of the Liberal-Agrarian coalition of 1950. A voluntary system was to be reconstructed in which all people would be free to choose whether or not they would take advantage of the health insurance available and in which commonwealth benefits would depend on a person's being insured by a qualified health insurance plan. Deeble speculated that the Australian voluntary insurance system succeeded politically for so long "because it offered advantages to all of the participating parties—the doctors, the commonwealth government, the state government, and the subscribers—without imposing binding obligations on any one of them."[16] In this connection he observed that in 1982, 50 percent of all funding that passed through the voluntary health insurance funds ultimately came from government insurance, nearly 20 percent in direct subsidies and about 30 percent in tax concessions.[17]

In the election campaign of 1983 health insurance became one of the clearest issues of difference between the parties. On March 5, 1983, the Labour party swept into office. Labour representatives had promised during the election campaign to return to a universal, tax-funded health insurance scheme based on a single public source of funds allowing for greater fiscal control and equity in sharing costs. Labour renamed this proposal Medicare, emulating Canada's rubric. (In the United States, the term Medicare applies to insurance for people 65 years of age or over.) The Australian Medicare differs from the original Labour party Medibank I by being substantially funded through a 1 percent levy on personal income, together with a revision of the health insurance subsidies existing before its introduction. Private insurers were able to offer forms of insurance supplementing Medicare, but were forbidden to insure the gap between physicians' fees and the government-allowed fee schedule. Such is the current status of the Australian health service delivery system and health insurance. There appears to be as yet no direct attack on the structure of the delivery system, but if the Labour party stays in power long enough, it is reasonable to assume that moves will be made in that direction also.

Given the fluid nature of Australian political propensities, it will be of interest to follow developments. If Thelma Hunter's description of the Australian political process holds true, intense wheeling and dealing will continue. She observed, for example, that during the debate on the Jamison Report between December 30, 1980, and April 13, 1981, there was a split in the Cabinet, eight Cabinet discussions, 11 task force meetings, three working party meetings, seven memoranda to the Cabinet, nine submissions of the minister of health, and more than 14 hours of Cabinet time.[18]

Colin Burrows remarked in 1987 that if the Labour government retains office—and as of mid-1988 it has—it is likely that the existing comprehensive, centralized, and universal health insurance system will continue. He remarked further, however, that "If as seems likely, the conservative coalition is returned to power, it is difficult to predict what will happen. There will be less emphasis on direct control of costs because of the commitment to market forces as the primary control mechanism." The result will be "another round of changes and adjustments because there is little in the evidence of history that a politically and economically viable health system can operate in Australia through the medium of voluntary insurance and fee-for-services health care delivery."[19] This would appear to be a reasonable conclusion, but Australia, like the United States, is so far collectively unable to make up its mind.

Summary

I place Australia to the left of the United States in the market-minimized/market-maximized continuum because it has a universal health insurance plan, but still the Australian system is so pluralistic that it could be placed parallel to the United States or to its right. In any case, they are very close to each other and stand out almost apart from the other countries covered in this book. Since the Labour government is staying in power, perhaps there will be some stability in the current health insurance situation. Still, Australian politics and society are so volatile that a return to Liberal-Agrarian Government may once again change this seeming stability.

Notes

1. Sidney Sax, *The Strife of Interests, Politics and Policies in Australian Health Services* (Sydney: Allen and Unwin, 1984), p. 6.
2. Ibid., p. 15.
3. C. Thame, "Health and the State: The Development of Collective Responsibility for Health Care in the First Half of the Twentieth Century" (Ph.D. diss., Australian National University, Canberra, 1974).

4. Sax, *The Strife of Interests*, p. 26.
5. Ibid., p. 27.
6. R. B. Scotton and J. Deeble, "Compulsory Health Insurance of Australia," *Australian Economic Review*, Fourth Quarter (1968): 9–16.
7. Sax, *The Strife of Interests*, p. 92.
8. Ibid., p. 115.
9. Odin W. Anderson, Personal Memorandum, unpublished, 1976. I was a guest of the Australian Hospital Association for 12 days to address its annual conference in Sydney. In turn the association facilitated a dozen or so interviews with leading pertinent informants on the Australian health services spectrum.
10. Sax, *The Strife of Interests*, p. 131.
11. Commission of Inquiry into the Efficiency and Administration of Hospitals (Canberra: Australian Government Printing Service, 1981).
12. Ibid., p. 48.
13. Ibid., p. 49.
14. Ibid., p. 61.
15. Ibid., p. 57.
16. John S. Deeble, "Unscrambling the Omlet: Public and Private Health Care Financing in Australia," in *The Public and Private Mix for Health: The Relevance and Effects of Change*, ed. Gordon McLachlan and Alan Maynard (London: Nuffield Provincial Hospitals and Trust, 1982), p. 452.
17. Ibid., p. 457.
18. Thelma Hunter, "The Politics of National Health Insurance: Plus Change?" in *Perspectives on Health Policy*, ed. P. Michael Tatchell. Proceedings of a Public Affairs Conference held at the Australian National University, July 2, 1982. (Canberra: Australian National University, Health Economics Research Unit, 1984) p. 29. There are other other good articles in this publication. Other sources on the Australian Health Services read for background but not cited directly are: Thelma Hunter, "Medical Politics: Decline in the Hegemony of the Australian Medical Association?" *Social Science & Medicine* 18 (1984): 973–80; Michael Tatchell, "A Comparative Examination of the Australian and New Zealand Health Systems," in *Community Health Studies VI* (Canberra: Australian National University, Health Economics Research Unit, Reprint Series 8, 1982), pp. 274–91; L. J. Opit, "The Cost of Health Care and Health Insurance in Australia: Some Problems Associated with the Fee-for-Service System," *Social Science & Medicine* 18 (1984): 967–72; Errol Pickering, "Caring for the Aged in Australia," *World Hospitals* 19 (April 1983): 22–24; John Dewdney, "Australia," in *Comparative Health Systems: Descriptive Analyses of Fourteen National Health Systems*, ed. Marshall W. Raffel (University Park, PA: Pennsylvania State University Press, 1984), pp. 1–54; J. M. Najmam and J. S. Western, "A Comparative Analysis of Australian Health Policy in the 1970s," *Social Science & Medicine* 18 (1984): 949–58; Malcolm C. Brown, *National Health Insurance in Canada and Australia: A Comparative Political Economy Analysis*. A study by the Health Economics Research Unit in association with the Center for Research on Federal Financial Relations (Canberra: Australian National University, Health Economics Research Unit, Research Monograph 3, 1983); S. J. Duckett, "Structural Interests and Australian Health Policy," *Social Science & Medicine* 18 (1984): 959–66.
19. Colin Burrows, "The Ever Changing Australian Health Care System: A Problem of Structure and Ideology." Unpublished paper delivered at the Workshop in Health Administration Studies, University of Chicago, February 12, 1987.

Chapter 8

The United States

Personal health services have been a growth enterprise in the United States since 1875.[1] The enterprise has taken place essentially in the private sector of the economy, through a mixture of non-profit and for-profit firms, with increasing government support and intervention. This mixture has changed over the years, primarily in regard to sources of income for day-to-day operations and capital funding. Americans manifest a great deal of ambivalence about who is responsible for health care, the individual or the government. Collective solutions have received mixed reactions: life insurance, fire insurance, and community fund drives for hospital construction were easily accepted a long time ago, but private health insurance made no headway until people recognized that, like life and fire insurance, it was a prudent way to protect their solvency. Medical care for the poor was regarded as an expression of the noblesse oblige of the physician and the hospital, buttressed by local government and philanthropic organizations.

The personal health services system seems to fall naturally into three major stages of development: 1875 to 1930, 1930 to 1965, and 1965 to the present. These stages are briefly presented, with some attention given to public health services and mental hospitals which preceded and then paralleled the growth of personal health services.

1875–1930

In the United States during the later part of the nineteenth century, physicians and pharmacists were the sole dispensers of professionally recognized health services. On the periphery were midwives, who, by the turn of the century, were beginning to be replaced by physicians. Also on the periphery were doctors of osteopathy, chiropractors, and others. Dentists developed a separate, parallel profession.

The general hospital as we know it today did not exist. Poorhouses and almshouses took care of the destitute and persons who had no family. Illnesses were treated primarily in patients' homes and physicians' offices. Physicians and pharmacists were entrepreneurs, presumably with a code of ethics and professional standards. They were not motivated strictly by profit and had an implied obligation to persons unable to pay. There were proportionately as many physicians then as there are now. They made their living treating patients for fees and received very little income from government or philanthropic sources. To my knowledge, in no other country have so many physicians and dentists been supported by private, fee-for-service patients. The same was true of pharmacists, who eventually established the peculiarly American "corner drugstore" to supplement their income from prescriptions. Private practice and fee-for-service thus became firmly embedded in American medical care.

Surgery had become highly developed by 1875 because of operations performed in the charity hospitals of the East Coast and Europe. At the time, the middle and upper classes would not have been caught dead in these famous hospitals, but that changed with the advent of anesthesia and antisepsis, which made the general hospital a relatively safe and painless place for surgery. The affluent began to seek the service of surgeons, who in turn sought hospital admitting privileges. By 1900 there were 4,000 general hospitals in the United States, whereas there had been only a few score in 1875.

Hospitals were established by voluntary community boards and church bodies. The church bodies, of course, had a long history of caring for the poor, and capital came from the millionaires created by the tremendous industrial development following the Civil War. Only a small minority of general hospitals were built for the poor by municipalities. Voluntary hospitals, because of their charitable and nonprofit charters, were obliged to provide care for the poor who sought help, but by and large the poor were a minority of their patients. The burgeoning economy enabled hospitals to obtain capital funds from philanthropists and operating funds from paying patients. Physicians, particularly those who wanted to perform surgery, made arrangements with the hospitals to admit their private patients. These patients would pay the hospital's charges and the surgeon's fees. In return, the surgeons were provided a free workshop in which to provide free care for the poor, an ideal symbiotic arrangement. American society has a long tradition of voluntary self-help on the community level, and the voluntary hospitals are prime examples of this tradition. The nurturing functions of the family found expression in the voluntary hospital when the home became unequal to the increasingly technical demands of medicine.

The trained nurse, in cap and uniform, functioned as the physician's assistant. The popularized view of Florence Nightingale was an attractive model, and the nursing profession became an alternative to teaching and secretarial positions for women; it was possibly more honored because of its emphasis on service. Nurses' hours were long and their pay low, mostly in kind.

Dentists, like physicians, were entrepreneurs, who made their way by fees from private patients. Since the public was indifferent to matters of dental health then, the services of dentists were not in great demand. Dentistry, like medicine, benefitted greatly from the advent of anesthesia and antisepsis.

Up to the end of the nineteenth century, most physicians were trained through apprenticeships with practicing physicians. There were also so-called diploma mills, which were established by physicians to train several students at a time in rather primitive arrangements. Later, private and public universities established medical schools. Dentists also had proprietary schools initially and then eventually schools in universities. Nurses were trained by hospitals, which benefitted from the inexpensive labor of student nurses and exercised virtually total supervision over them. As medical science advanced, a variety of other types of personnel began to appear.

All this took money, but money became available with the growth of the economy. The surplus was increasingly poured into personal health services, which, until the 1930s, Americans bought without the help of government or private insurance. Thus the infrastructure of the personal health services as we know them today—the voluntary hospital and privately practicing physicians, dentists, and pharmacists—was in place by the 1930s.

Public health services and mental hospitals were not desired to the same extent as personal health services. Before 1875, cities and counties had begun to establish health departments because effluents were contaminating the water and causing epidemics of cholera. Later, when communicable diseases in children could be controlled by immunization and pasteurization, the health department expanded its functions based on bacteriology and epidemiology. Public health training was added to the registered nurse's curriculum to create public health nurses for mothers and infants. Public health separated itself early from the private practice of medicine. Public health officers were not allowed to practice medicine, following the English model.

The building of mental hospitals (usually out in the country) preceded the development of personal health services. Mental hospitals were and continue to be more or less separate from personal health services. They were and are largely publicly owned and operated. Like public health departments, they are not highly valued, judging from the public funding they receive compared to the magnitude of the problems they deal with. Personal health services, through sheer demand and popularity, have cornered the available funding.

This was the situation in 1930. The system was shaped by hospital owners, physicians, and philanthropists. Government, except by issuing licenses and setting standards did not influence the structure of the system. The public presumably approved of the structure because people used and paid for it in increasing numbers. The government helped the system indirectly by permitting hospitals to be tax-exempt enterprises. In addition, capital gifts to hospitals were tax-exempt. In other words, the private sector subsidized the construction of hospitals, an interesting mixture of nonprofit and for-profit enterprise that was accepted by the body politic as natural. Personal health services, which are oriented toward acute care, were stimulated enormously by the dynamics of medical science, technology, and money. In the 1930s, this system was poised for the even more dynamic expansion that it has experienced since. Relative to personal health services, public health departments and mental hospitals have barely held their own.

1930–1965

While the period from 1875 to 1930 witnessed the development of the health services infrastructure, the period from 1930 to 1965 is characterized mainly by the emergence of a third party to pay the day-to-day expenses. The rise of the third-party payers was undoubtedly stimulated by the depression of the 1930s, when both hospital and personal income fell, but it is likely that the third party would have emerged anyway. Hospitals could operate better with a steady income, and families could more readily meet the increasing costs resulting from improved medical technology. Hospitals began to sponsor prepayment plans, which eventually became known as Blue Cross plans. After 1933, the health services resumed their growth, as reflected in the proportion of the gross national product directed to them. Hospital stays were relative costly and lent themselves well to insurance, since a fairly predictable number of individuals in the population would incur hospital expenses in a year.

In the late 1930s, prepayment plans for physicians' services in the hospital, mainly surgery, also began to appear. Sponsored by the state medical societies, these became known as Blue Shield plans. Surgery was a relatively expensive procedure that lent itself to the concept of insurance. State governments continued to sponsor health services for the poor, and eventually a shared program between the federal government and the states emerged.

During the 1940s and into World War II, private insurance companies discovered from the experience of Blue Cross and Blue Shield plans that hospital care and surgery were insurable. Congress gave the voluntary plans a financial boost by decreeing that health insurance (and pensions) were fringe benefits and thus exempt from the wartime freeze on wages. This is another example of government encouragement of the private sector, since health insurance paid by the employer is a tax-exempt business expense. Further, signing up for fringe benefits became a condition of employment. This form of compulsion was acceptable, whereas any compulsory government program would have been taboo. After the passage of the 1935 Social Security Act, which mandated chiefly pensions and unemployment insurance, legislation proposing compulsory health insurance was put on Congress's back burner until 1952, the last year of Harry Truman's presidency.

The Blue Cross and Blue Shield plans and the private insurance companies were spectacularly successful. They went far beyond their own expectations in enrolling employee groups in the major industries, and by 1952, over one-half of the population was covered by some form of health insurance, mainly for hospital care and physician services in the hospital. With the election of Dwight Eisenhower in 1952, the venomous controversy over voluntary versus compulsory, government-sponsored health insurance subsided. Eisenhower would not support universal health insurance, and it became a dead political issue.

A salient aspect of the rise in third-party payers is that the organizational structure of health services that had emerged since 1875 was taken as a given; the insurance agencies and the government were concerned with paying its charges. In the case of hospitals, the concept was one of costs, and hospital accounting systems were underdeveloped and varied. Physicians were paid by voluntary health insurance according to prevailing fee schedules negotiated by Blue Shield plans, assuming there were any negotiations at all. There were no direct negotiations with private insurance companies because there were no contracts with them. These reimbursement methods seem irresponsible in retrospect, but money flowed freely then in a rapidly expanding economy. Public health departments exhorted the public to "see your doctor early" and promoted maternal and child health programs. Encouragement was scarcely needed for either major or minor surgery. Admissions to hospitals and visits to physicians increased dramatically between the late 1930s and the 1960s: hospital admissions increased from 90 per 1,000 persons in the population per year to 145; the percentage of the population who saw a physician in a year increased from 39 to 65. The supply of hospital beds and physicians increased more or less in relation to demand. Physicians became very busy and prosperous. Hospital occupancy rates went up, and hospitals also became prosperous, their chronic deficits notwithstanding, deficits being a symbol of charity.

To add to the stock of hospitals and beds, particularly in rural areas,

Congress in 1946 passed the Hospital Survey and Construction (Hill-Burton) Act. This act was supported by such diverse interests as a American Hospital Association, the American Medical Association, and labor organizations, which ordinarily worked at cross-purposes in efforts to enact government health insurance. The act was designed as a one-time grant to hospitals, both public and voluntary, for start-up costs, with grant funds to be matched by the hospitals. Each state for the first time took an inventory of its hospital beds, and grants were made to hospitals within the framework of a loose plan. The act supplied about 25 percent of the expenditures for hospitals, which in turn generated a considerable amount of money from public and, mainly, private sources. The main object of the act, which was very successful, was to buttress the voluntary hospital. The old sources of capital, philanthropy and community fund-raising drives, were diminishing, and public hospitals were regarded as outside the mainstream of the hospital system. This is another instance of government's supporting the private nonprofit sector. The voluntary hospital was an integral part of community life and interwove the private and public sectors so closely as to make it difficult to differentiate between them.

By the early 1950s, an engine of finance had been established from private sources for the day-to-day operation of the hospital and physician services and from public and private sources for the supply of hospital beds, physicians, and other personnel. The general economy and the health services economy were booming. The existing health services infrastructure continued to be accepted as a given.

Within the relatively private, nonprofit health services economy, however, there was a development that was concerned directly with restructuring the delivery of physician services and hospital care. This was the group-practice prepayment plan, which attempted to compete with solo-practice, fee-for-service medical delivery, to engage a range of specialists on a salary, to provide a full range of physician services, from curative to preventive, and to serve a known population. The Kaiser-Permanente plans were established in the West, and the Health Insurance Plan of Greater New York was established in the East. In cities like Washington, D.C., Seattle, St. Louis, and Minneapolis—St. Paul, similar plans were established on a more or less cooperative, consumer-owned basis. Initially, medical societies' opposition to these new arrangements were fierce. Gradually, however, the group-practice prepayment plans began to take their place in the spectrum of types of health services delivery, and in some areas they became options in labor-management negotiations for fringe benefits. Their influence appeared to be out of all proportion to their pace of growth (involving about 4 percent of the population), since they became reference points for quality health services at a "reasonable" price. It seems that only in the United States was this diversity of delivery types possible. American physicians have an entrepreneurial propensity and an ability to raise capital unlike physicians in any other country. The concept of private group practices that charge fees undoubtedly inspired the concept of group-practice prepayment in which physicians live on premiums divided among the physicians on salaries.

The private engine of finance was aided by the public engine with the passage of the Medicare Act for the elderly and the Medicaid Act for the poor in 1965. Medicare is a federal program, and Medicaid is a shared federal-state program. Medicare takes the cost of care of the aged off the backs of families and the private sector, and Medicaid, along with assuaging the national conscience, takes the cost of care of the poor off the shaky revenue structure of the states and tries to equalize care for the poor across states. By 1965, private and nonprofit insurance agencies were supplying 40 percent of the cost of day-to-day operations of hospitals and 30 percent of physician services. Government, mainly the federal government, was paying for 50 percent of the hospital costs and 20 percent of physician services.

The stage was set for a spectacular increase in price and use. There were no serious built-in controls on costs. The health services enterprise had become accustomed to being paid what it asked, and the funding services did not demur because employees, employers, and Congress did not demur either. From 1950 to 1965, expenditures as a percentage of the gross national product rose from 4.6 to 5.9. Expenditures per capita for all services rose from $78 to $198, not accounting for inflation, which was moderate during that period. The private insurance agencies and the government teamed up to assure a health service where cost would be of no consequence.

Concomitantly, the proportion of people age 65 and over was increasing, particularly those 75 to 80 and over. Associated with aging are chronic illness and disability and the increasing financial helplessness that overtakes families with aged members. By the 1950s, expenditures on nursing homes had become a visible portion of the national medical dollar, but only a small portion of this cost could be expected from direct-pay patients. Public medical assistance for the indigent in nursing homes became a prime source of funding for day-to-day operations, and Medicaid buttressed it greatly after 1965. True to the American tradition, the market for nursing homes was met primarily by the private sector, both for-profit and nonprofit, and standards were set by the states together with Medicaid and Medicare. Government was unable or unwilling to supply enough nursing home beds to meet the demand and need. As usual, government bought services from the private sector and paid pretty much what the nursing homes were charging.

1965 to the Present

It was not until the late 1960s that the big buyers of services—government, employers and labor unions, and insurance and prepayment agencies—began to be generally concerned over rising expenditures for personal health services. They found the pace of the increase that alarming, with costs rising faster than the general economy as reflected in the consumer price index and the gross national product. The public was primarily interested in reducing out-of-pocket expenditures, and the buyers of services were interested in keeping insurance premiums and reimbursements to providers low. Hospital expenditures were rising at the dizzying pace of 15 percent annually. Expenditures for physician services were not far behind. Providers said the increases in expenditures were justified in large part because of improved services and increased use, as well as rising labor costs in a labor-intensive enterprise. No one knew what constituted an appropriate level of expenditures, but there seemed to be general agreement that the current level was too high. Theories of costs and expenditures were primitive.

This period, then, was characterized by an intense concern with how to manage the health services enterprise so that buyers knew what they were buying and providers knew what they were offering. The practice of simply paying what the providers asked was being seriously questioned. Further, the payment mechanism was to be used to manage the system. Three methods of doing so emerged, largely in this order: (1) monitoring physician decision making in hospitals, (2) control of hospital beds, and (3) control of hospital reimbursement rates.

Attempts at rationalizing the personal health services were expressed mainly in group-practice prepayment plans. These were set up not simply to save money but also to provide comprehensive services efficiently and conveniently. It seemed that saving money was a secondary although acknowledged consideration. Likewise, the scores of hospital planning councils that were established in major cities, sponsored by local hospitals and funded in large part by the then Department of Health, Education and Welfare, were aimed less at saving money than at systematizing hospital relationships and cooperation on the local level. The councils were intended to serve as information clearinghouses on hospital beds and equipment in local areas, the presumption being that the hospitals would recognize their own interest. These councils may have had other effects, but the evidence shows that reducing duplication of services and stabilizing the bed supply were not among them.

The lack of success of the hospital council concept led to the federal program called Comprehensive Health Planning. This program was to be concerned with facilities planning through the states and incorporated many of the hospital planning councils as agents of the state. Another federal endeavor through the state at this time, the Regional Medical Programs, was aimed at delivery of services for heart disease, cancer, stroke, and related diseases. It attempted to connect practicing physicians to medical schools and major medical centers so that physicians could benefit from the latest knowledge concerning these diseases and refer their patients more appropriately. Saving money was not the primary concern; integrating physician services was. Both Comprehensive Health Planning and the Regional Medical Programs failed in terms of the nonexistent performance standards implicit, but certainly not explicit, in the legislation. In the meantime, expenditures increased apace; the internal and external dynamics of this tremendous growth enterprise were awesome. Two prestigious government commissions were formed, one in 1968 on hospital effectiveness and one in 1970 on Medicaid and medical care for the poor, the latter actually expanding its vague charge to consider the entire delivery structure and planning. The tone in both reports was confusion and frustration, as well it might be: the commissions were ambiguous about planning, although advocating it, and distressed by the prospect of further government intervention, although helpless to suggest anything else. The Medicaid report did begin to refer to competition among delivery systems as a means of containing rising expenditures.

More specific attempts at containing expenditures, however, were made in the Medicare Act, and they also applied to Medicaid. The act mandated reviews of physician decisions regarding length of stay in hospitals—that is, direct monitoring of professional decision making. From the profession's viewpoint, this was a radical step.

On the state level, legislatures began to pass laws calling for certificates of need for hospital beds. The building of new hospitals and the expansion or renovation of old hospitals had to be approved by a state planning agency, a control on supply. State legislatures also began to regulate hospital rate setting, a control on price.

As a result of its 1965 mandate, Congress passed a law in 1972 requiring utilization review of hospital care (that is, physician decision making) on an areawide basis by committees of physicians. These groups were called professional standards review organizations. To cap all these developments, Congress passed the National Health Planning and Resources Development Act in 1974, mandating the creation of over 200 health planning areas. These were administered by health services agencies, whose boards of governors were made up primarily of consumers. Consumers were to be appointed on the basis of race, ethnic background, income, and geographic area. The health services agencies were to determine the appropriateness of hospital construction, distribution, and renovation and of the acquisition policies of hospitals regarding expensive equipment. Further, the health services agencies were to work up master plans of the health needs in their areas according to federal guidelines. Plans were then passed on to the appropriate state and federal agencies for review and consideration.

Congress intended to place determination of needs and control over the construction of facilities on the local level. Local needs determined by health services agencies would be communicated to upper levels of government, particularly the federal government, which could then negotiate on long-term basis. Congress and perhaps even the bureaucracy are exceedingly chary of imposing a blueprint on the states and local areas, preferring instead to set up fairly loose guidelines for discussion to reach consensus. It was apparently Congress's intent to put a planning apparatus in place before the enactment of some form of national health insurance, in order to have a handle on costs and to direct the development of personal health services. Certification of need and rate control, although functions of the states, were delegated to the health services agencies for recommendations and were therefore a concern of the federal government, which could withhold payment from hospitals that did not comply. Even so, the planning apparatus did not have a firm place in national policy and continued to exist on sufferance on very slender appropriations. It lasted from 1974 to 1983. The Reagan administration abolished it with no political repercussions. It had no viable political support.

Americans tend to look suspiciously at structures, boundaries, and budget caps. It was hoped that the monitoring of physician decision making would lead to a rational, justifiable volume and quality of services at reasonable costs within the planning framework briefly described here. A more recent effort to curtail escalating costs is the health maintenance organization. Old as a concept but relatively new in terms of government support, health maintenance organizations embody prepayment plans that attempt to monitor physician decision making, set a fixed premium for comprehensive services, and serve a known population. These plans have shown that they use hospital services less than the fee-for-service system and hence tend to cost less. Competition is thus being carried over to health services delivery, encouraging a choice of plans among employed groups in hopes of tempering the rise in health services costs.

In the meantime, despite professional standards review organizations, certification of need, state review, and planning, the personal health services economy is growing, expenditures continue to rise, and attempts to manage the system do not seem to have had much effect as yet. Between 1965 and 1984, the percentage of the gross national product spent for all health services increased from 5.9 to 10.5, per capita expenditures increased from $198 to $1,600, and the trend is clearly up. The ultimate weapon, of course, is in the hands of big buyers of the services, who can refuse to provide more money. The pluralistic nature of funding, however, makes such a course difficult, even though the federal government is now the source of 40 percent of all expenditures for personal health services. Under the Reagan administration, Congress authorized budget caps on payments to physicians and hospitals. Expenditures are still rising, but at a somewhat slower pace.

Some years ago I wrote a book on the private and public financing of the personal health services, called *The Uneasy Equilibrium*. The uneasy equilibrium between private and public control and financing continues, but in a much more intense form. The government still does not own and does not want to own, the hospitals. It does not want to make physicians into salaried employees. The private sector, if it is politically astute, is playing on Congress's reluctance to set up a highly structured system. The private sector may well continue to be an effective balance against government intervention—a term implying that government is intervening in an otherwise normal situation—because the American people want choices, easy access, and the latest technology rather than low cost. To the public, the relationship of health services expenditures to the gross national product is an abstraction that has no bearing on daily life.

Political rhetoric supports health care as a right, but political factions differ on what constitutes equity of access to personal health services. Medicaid for the very poor appears to be the standard of equity so far. But eligibility standards for Medicaid are being lowered in order to reduce the population eligible, thus enlarging the number of people not insured. There is increasing political interest in covering the uninsured, who are estimated to make up around 12 percent of the population. The Reagan administration established a fiscal policy rather than a health policy to curb the costs of health services. The major method used was to sanction the growth of health maintenance organizations so that groups of doctors could compete with each other and with the mainstream fee-for-service and insurance system. Employers facilitated competitive options among their employees. About 10 to 12 percent of the population is currently enrolled in health maintenance organizations with the percentage varying considerably between areas. For example, Minneapolis–St. Paul health maintenance organizations cover 50 percent of the market of two million people.

Overall, a great mixture of methods is in place to contain costs, showing the difficulty of instituting precise controls. Among the methods are regulation of hospital bed supply, regulation of hospital charges, higher deductibles and coinsurance for patients with insurance, and the formation of coalitions of business and industrial firms as collective bargaining agencies with providers. The government has frozen physician fees for Medicare and instituted flat cost estimates by diagnosis for hospital care. A prospective "glut" of physicians may increase the possibility of harder bargaining with physicians by health maintenance organizations and insurance agencies, leading to more controlled costs. Last, to give competition free play, the National Health Planning and Resources Development Act has been abolished.

The American health care services have been cut loose in an open field in a way that no other country has conceived of or dared to try. The concepts of nonprofit and profit are being blurred. The sheer magnitude of expenditures has spawned business management concepts and methods. Still, there is a general uneasiness as to the future shape of the U.S. health services. A massive experiment is taking place limited to the objective of containing costs.

Summary

It takes little agonizing to place the United States in the market-minimized/market-maximized continuum. There is no universal health insurance plan. The governments—federal, state, and local—run only a minority of the hospitals. Health services entitlements are limited to Medicare for the elderly and Medicaid for the poor. The Veteran's Administration program, which should also be mentioned in this connection, is theoretically limited to service-connected diseases and disabilities and accounts for only around 5 percent of the country's total health services expenditures. (A British visitor once told me before Medicare that we have socialized medicine only for heroes.) There is comparatively extreme pluralism as to ownership of hospitals, types of health insurance, and sources of funding. The country is ideologically anchored in private enterprise in the health services although there are many pragmatic accommodations within that ideology. One is an employer's stipulation that an employee must enroll in labor-management negotiated health insurance as a condition of employment, an indirect form of compulsion. Another is that employers may deduct their contributions to health insurance from their corporate business expenses, a hidden subsidy on the part of government. There are others, but these stand out.

Note

1. The sources for this chapter on the United States are too numerous to set forth in detail. I believe adequate documentation can be found for this synthesis in my work starting with: *The Uneasy Equilibrium: Private and Public Financing of Health Services in the United States 1875–1965* (New Haven, CT: College and University Press, 1968); *Blue Cross Since 1929* (Cambridge, MA: Ballinger, 1975); and *Health Services in the United States: A Growth Enterprise Since 1875* (Ann Arbor, MI: Health Administration Press, 1985); and with others, *HMO Development: Patterns and Prospects; A Comparative Analysis of HMOs*, University of Chicago, Center for Health Administration Studies, Research Series No. 32 (Chicago: Pluribus Press, 1985).

Part III

Management and Control

Chapter 9

Operational and Performance Indicators

T he preceding historical case studies have attempted to show the similarities and differences in the development of the health services delivery systems in the selected countries and to suggest some reasons for the similarities and differences. Secondary data sources of a nonstatistical nature have been quite adequate for the purpose of delineating the macro characteristics of the respective systems. The statistics on long-term as well as current trends of operational and performance indicators are, however, quite inadequate for proper understanding and evaluation of the operation and performance of the selected delivery systems. The most that can be gleaned from them is a sense of the range of differences in the supply and use of facilities and personnel, in national expenditures as a percentage of gross domestic product (GDP), in total aggregate and per capita expenditures for all health services (frequently by components of services), and in the proportions of expenditures coming from public and private sources.

It is of interest that the United States has probably more complete statistical information on the operation and performance of its comparatively pluralistic system than does any other country, dating back to 1929 when the Department of Commerce began to collect annual data on total national expenditures. All countries become interested in knowing what they are doing after their health services delivery systems are well in place, but no country gathered data for the purpose of planning and directing the development of its health services. The United States, however, started early to conduct primary and systematic research on consumer use and expenditure patterns and to examine different types of organizational study.[1] (Indeed, 30 years ago, when the British National Health Service had been in operation for a decade while the United States continued debating private versus national health insurance, a British colleague, Louis Moss, remarked to me that Great Britain had a policy but no data, whereas the United States had data but no policy.) Regrettably, the solutions that should have been self-evident from the gathered data foundered against political interest groups. Still, interest groups desired data in order to justify their policies and proposals as is true in all countries.

The statistical data in this chapter are drawn from the 1985 and 1987 reports of the Organization for Economic Cooperation and Development (OECD).[2] These reports covered 24 developed countries, including the 7 countries selected for this book.

Financing

The favorite figure used to compare countries' expenditures for health services is the gross domestic product—the total expenditure for all goods and services in a country for a year. Table 1 presents health services expenditures as a percentage of the 1984 GDP for the countries under study, with the countries ordered according to their positions in the market-minimized/market-maximized continuum: market-minimized at the top of the list and market-maximized at the bottom. While this sample is too small for valid generalizations, there are too few developed countries to justify running correlations in any case. As seen in the right-hand column, there is a rough relationship between the percentage of total health expenditures coming from public funding sources and location in the continuum. The United Kingdom and Sweden are high in their proportion of expenditures from public sources, and the United States is conspicuously low. Among the others, France is relatively low. All countries except the United States cover hospital and physician services. The United Kingdom and Sweden provide the most comprehensive range of health care services of these seven countries, a fact reflected in the percentages of health services expenditures that come from their public funds.

There does not seem to be any pattern in this small sample as to the relationship between a country's position in the market-minimized/market-maximized continuum and its total expenditures on health as a percentage of GDP. The United Kingdom and the United States, the extremes of the market-minimized/market-maximized continuum, represent also the extremes of total expenditures on health. But Sweden, which is next to the United Kingdom in market minimization, has a GDP expenditure on health second only to that of the United States. France, a rather pluralistic system, also has high expenditures. There are too many unknown variables entering into the percentage of GDP devoted to health expenditures to make any sense of the middle column in Table 1.

To what extent are health expenditures as a percentage of GDP a function of the magnitude of each country's GDP? The United States and Sweden, for example, have considerably higher living standards than the United Kingdom. It could therefore be said that the United Kingdom in relation to its economic level is spending more on health services than either the United States or Sweden. Can these relationships be unscrambled? Economists have difficulties in doing so, but the book by Robert Maxwell and the OECD report are candid in explaining the difficulties, and at least we are trying to reveal the state of the art.[3]

Table 2 is also intriguing and simplistically descriptive. It shows that the compound annual rate of growth in health services expenditures in the United Kingdom is not grossly different from the rates of the other countries in this study even though the United Kingdom's health services expenditures as a percentage of GDP are appreciably lower. This fact may cast some doubt on the United Kingdom's ability to control health services costs to the extent to which it is credited with doing so. The dynamics of increases in health services expenditures is universal. There appears to be a gradual increase in the compound rate of growth in these expenditures from the market-minimized United Kingdom to the market-maximized United States.

Table 1: Total Expenditures on Health as a Percentage of Gross Domestic Product and Public Expenditures on Health as a Percentage of Total Expenditures on Health, 1984

	Total Expenditures on Health as a Percentage of GDP	*Public Expenditures on Health as a Percentage of Total Expenditures on Health*
United Kingdom	5.9	88.9
Sweden	9.4	91.4
Canada	8.4	74.4
West Germany	8.1	78.2
France	9.1	71.2
Australia	7.8	84.5
United States	10.7	41.4

Source: Organization for Economic Cooperation and Development, *Financing and Delivering Health Care: A Comparative Analysis of OECD Countries*, Social Policy Studies No. 4 (Paris: The Organization, 1987), p. 55.

Table 2: Compound Annual Rate of Growth in Health
Services Expenditures, 1970–1984

United Kingdom	10.6
Sweden	10.5
Canada	10.3
West Germany	12.0
France	12.4
Australia	11.0
United States	11.3

Source: Organization for Economic Cooperation and Development,
*Financing and Delivering Health Care: A Comparative Analysis of
OECD Countries*, Social Policy Studies No. 4 (Paris: The Organization,
1987), p. 56.

Table 3 shows 1984 per capita health services expenditures for the study
countries in U.S. dollars. When these figures are placed alongside the figures
for health services expenditures as a percentage of the GDP, the expected
relationship appears: countries whose health services expenditures account
for lower percentages of their GDPs have lower per capita health services
expenditures as well, and those with higher health services expenditures
relative to their GDPs have higher per capita health services expenditures.
The OECD report is very cautious about the methodology for comparing
"market baskets" of goods and services in general, not to mention health
services market baskets. Intuitively, however, the data appear to make sense.
     The whole world envies the United Kingdom its perceived ability to
control expenditures for health services better than other developed countries. That the United Kingdom is spending less per capita over time than
other countries is evident; that it is exerting superior control over expenditures needs qualification. Perhaps the United Kingdom started at a lower
base to begin with after World War II. The health services infrastructure
there was badly damaged but hardly more than that of West Germany or
France. The health services infrastructures of Sweden, Canada, Australia,
and the United States were not damaged at all, only slowed. In any case, an
annual compound growth rate of 10.6 percent would not seem to indicate
control. Other countries, including Sweden and Canada, have had slower
growth rates, although not low by any standards. The United Kingdom has
obviously been subjected to the same forces that tend to increase health
services expenditures as the other developed countries have and has responded similarly even within a highly structured delivery system with centralized financing and budget caps.
     Very capable economists made a recent and valiant attempt to explain
the wide differences in Canadian and U.S. expenditures for acute hospital

Table 3: Per Capita Expenditures on Health Services, 1984 (in 1984 U.S. dollars)

United Kingdom	658
Sweden	1,445
Canada	1,275
West Germany	1,079
France	1,145
Australia	994
United States	1,637

Source: Organization for Economic Cooperation and Development, *Financing and Delivering Health Care: A Comparative Analysis of OECD Countries*, Social Policy Studies No. 4 (Paris: The Organization, 1987), p. 56.

care from 1981 through 1985.[4] Taking into consideration admission rates, length of stay, and case mix for patients 65 years of age or over (since Canada and the United States are quite comparable in government health insurance for persons in this age range), the authors conclude that the appreciably higher U.S. expenditures on older patients are due to a greater intensity of care in the United States. Is this greater intensity of care worth the money in terms of outcome?

My conclusion is that increases in expenditures transcend organizational structure, ownership, and funding sources. This conclusion will bring little comfort to policymakers, planners, and administrators: it means that the health services delivery systems are essentially unmanageable and very difficult to control. The major control mechanism is the budget, which governments and private insurance agencies have been reluctant to use in a Draconian fashion, although all countries are attempting to do so in one way or another. Public demand is too great, as will be indicated by data on trends in supply of facilities and personnel and in utilization.

Supply

As revealed in Table 4, there was wide variation in the percentage of population increase among the seven study countries from 1960 to 1983. Obviously, the faster the increase in population, the more resources a country needs to allocate to health services to keep the supply of facilities and personnel constant relative to the population (assuming, of course, that the supply *should* be constant relative to the population). In this respect, the United Kingdom has had the smallest problem in that the population increased only 7 percent from 1960 to 1983, whereas the Australian popula-

Table 4: Population, 1960 and 1983, and Percentage of Increase

	1960 Population (in thousands)	1983 Population (in thousands)	Percentage of Increase
United Kingdom	52,559	56,377	27
Sweden	7,480	8,331	10
Canada	17,909	24,907	28
West Germany	55,585	61,421	10
France	45,684	54,438	16
Australia	10,547	15,369	31
United States	180,671	234,496	23

Source: Organization for Economic Cooperation and Development, *Measuring Health Care, 1960–1983: Expenditures, Costs and Performance,* Social Policy Studies No. 2 (Paris: The Organization, 1985), p. 154.

tion increased 31 percent, the Canadian population 28 percent, and the U.S. population 23 percent. As will be seen in subsequent tables, all countries' expenditures for health services exceeded their growth of population by varying magnitudes.

Table 5 shows the phenomenal increase in the number of practicing physicians per 1,000 population from 1960 to 1983. The lowest increases were those for the United Kingdom and the United States, which were very close, 30 percent and 32 percent, respectively. Sweden had a phenomenal increase of 154 percent stemming from a public policy to increase its physician supply from the lowest among the countries in the liberal-democratic developed countries; it is now the highest, having moved from .95 physicians per 1,000 population to 2.41 physicians per 1,000 population. West Germany is close behind with 2.38 physicians per 1,000 population. The range in supply of physicians is from 1.29 per 1,000 population in the United Kingdom to 2.41 per 1,000 population in Sweden, a difference of 1.12 physicians per 1,000 population. These data indicate that there can be great variations in the supply of physicians within what are, presumably, functioning health services delivery systems.

Normally, as is seen in Table 6, there are fewer dentists per 1,000 population than physicians. In all the study countries except one, West Germany, the number of dentists has increased relative to population since 1960, and Sweden has significantly more dentists per 1,000 population than the other countries.

The number of pharmacists, as shown in Table 7, has also increased relative to population, with the increase varying from 11 percent in the United States to 119 percent in Australia. France appears to be better supplied with pharmacists than the other countries. (It seems curious that data are not supplied for the United Kingdom.)

Table 5: Practicing Physicians per 1,000 Population, 1960 and 1983, and Percentage of Increase

	1960		1983		Percentage of Increase
United Kingdom	1.04	(1971)	1.29	(1981)	24
Sweden	.95		2.41		154
Canada	1.19	(1961)	1.96		65
West Germany	1.43		2.39	(1982)	69
France	.98		2.17		121
Australia	1.13	(1961)	2.01		78
United States	1.44		1.90	(1981)	32

Source: Organization for Economic Cooperation and Development, *Measuring Health Care, 1960–1983: Expenditures, Costs and Performance*, Social Policy Studies No. 2 (Paris: The Organization, 1985), calculated, p. 90.

Table 6: Practicing Dentists per 1,000 Population, 1960 and 1983, and Percentage of Increase

	1960		1983		Percentage of Increase
United Kingdom	0.29	(1974)	0.32	(1981)	10
Sweden	0.68		1.37		102
Canada	0.32		0.48		50
West Germany	0.58		0.55	(1982)	−5
France	0.45	(1971)	0.61		36
Australia	0.35	(1971)	0.38		9
United States	0.50		0.56	(1982)	12

Source: Organization for Economic Cooperation and Development, *Measuring Health Care, 1960–1983: Expenditures, Costs and Performance*, Social Policy Studies No. 2 (Paris: The Organization, 1985), calculated, p. 91.

Table 7: Active Pharmacists per 1,000 Population, 1960 and 1983, and Percentage of Increase

	1960		1983		Percentage of Increase
United Kingdom	NA		NA		NA
Sweden	0.30		0.47		57
Canada	0.50		0.70	(1982)	40
West Germany	0.28		0.48	(1982)	71
France	0.56		0.76		36
Australia	0.16		0.35	(1981)	119
United States	0.56		0.62	(1980)	11

Source: Organization for Economic Cooperation and Development, *Measuring Health Care, 1960–1983: Expenditures, Costs and Performance*, Social Policy Studies No. 2 (Paris: The Organization, 1985), calculated, p. 93.

Table 8 shows the great increase in the number of professional and auxiliary nurses and midwives in the study countries since 1960. (Midwives are presumably nurses by training.) France has the fewest nurses relative to population, with 5.14 per 1,000 population and Canada the most, with 8.63 per 1,000 population, followed by the United Kingdom with 8.42 per 1,000 population. All countries claim that the supply of nurses is not adequate.

From Table 9 it is obvious that total employment in the health care field increased appreciably in the study countries from 1960 to 1983. Increases ranged from 76 percent in West Germany to 176 percent in Canada. Almost 4 percent of the population of Sweden (see Table 4) is employed in the health services, compared with about 1 percent of the population of West Germany. An appreciable proportion of the labor force in all countries is engaged in the health services, with the labor force generally making up around 60 percent of the population. Thus, in the United States, for example, it can be estimated that around 5 percent of the labor force is engaged in the health services, either in more or less direct service or supportive to those who are in direct care.

In Table 10 is seen the supply of beds in "medical institutions," to use the terminology of the OECD report. This category is a very crude one in that it does not separate short-term beds from long-term ones, which represent very variable per diem costs. The United States and Canada report quite accurately the differentiation between acute and long-term hospital beds, but the other five study countries give the impression that there are so many long-term patients in acute hospital beds as to make comparisons analytically difficult. Hence, OECD has lumped all beds into one category. Even this gross category reveals interesting differences. As has been known, among the liberal-democratic countries Sweden has the greatest number of beds per 1,000 population, remaining virtually constant at around 14. In 1983 the United States had the lowest ratio. Canada had a very high proportion of all beds in the acute category compared to the United States. Only the United Kingdom and the United States decreased their number of beds between 1960 and 1983. The reduction of beds in the United States by 37 percent in this period must be explained largely by the reduction of beds in psychiatric hospitals. This may also be true for the United Kingdom, which experienced an overall drop of 16 percent. Still, acute bed capacity is shrinking in the United States and the United Kingdom as a result of policy or as a result of lower hospital use for one reason or another.

The last illustrative table on supply is Table 11, which reports staff per bed, exclusive of physicians. Here again, there is a remarkable range: the number of nonphysician staff per bed varies from 1.14 in West Germany, to 3.27 in Australia. The United States and Canada are also on the high side, with 2.69 and 2.13 staff per bed, respectively, but no country's staffing approaches Australia's.

Table 8: Professional Nurses, Auxiliary Nurses, and Midwives per 1,000 Population, 1960 and 1983, and Percentage of Increase

	1960		*1983*		*Percentage of Increase*
United Kingdom	6.53	(1971)	8.42	(1981)	29
Sweden	3.09		7.99		158
Canada	6.05	(1966)	8.63	(1982)	24
West Germany	2.06		3.46	(1982)	68
France	3.31	(1971)	5.14		55
Australia	1.62		7.25		348
United States	2.92		5.43	(1980)	86

Source: Organization for Economic Cooperation and Development, *Measuring Health Care, 1960–1983: Expenditures, Costs and Performance*, Social Policy Studies No. 2 (Paris: The Organization, 1985), calculated, p. 92.

Table 9: Health Services Employees per 1,000 Population, 1960 and 1983, and Percentage of Increase

	1960		*1983*		*Percentage of Increase*
United Kingdom	10.94	(1961)	22.10		102
Sweden	15.64		39.49		152
Canada	7.76	(1961)	21.44	(1981)	176
West Germany	5.29		9.33	(1981)	76
France	9.59	(1971)	17.45		82
Australia	12.14	(1961)	29.69		136
United States	9.76		24.35		150

Source: Organization for Economic Cooperation and Development, *Measuring Health Care, 1960–1983: Expenditures, Costs and Performance*, Social Policy Studies No. 2 (Paris: The Organization, 1985), calculated, p. 89.

Utilization

As would be expected, data on rates of utilization of various types of service show considerable variation, as do those on expenditures and supply of facilities and personnel. Table 12 presents physician consultations per person per year. The countries selected for this book, with the exception of West Germany, exclude in-hospital visits from this category. (The OECD report does not so specify, but my general familiarity with physician consultation rates suggests that these figures must represent out-of-hospital visits only.) Between 1960 and the early 1980s, the number of physician consultations per person increased. Sweden had always had a remarkably low number of consultations per person, indicating some kind of constant factor in operation. There is speculation that perhaps Sweden's relatively high

Table 10: Medical Care Beds and Beds per 1,000 Population, 1960 and 1983, and Percentage of Increase

	1960		1983		
	Number of Beds	Beds per 1,000 Population	Number of Beds	Beds per 1,000 Population	Percentage of Increase
United Kingdom	543,457 (1961)	10.3	454,900 (1981)	8.7	−16
Sweden	102,394	13.7	116,688	14.0	2
Canada	110,829	6.2	170,538 (1982)	6.8	10
West Germany	583,513	10.5	683,624 (1982)	11.1	6
France	451,571 (1962)	9.9	632,644	11.6	17
Australia	98,923 (1962)	9.4	164,711 (1981)	10.7	14
United States	1,658,000	9.2	1,362,000 (1981)	5.8	−37

Source: Organization for Economic Cooperation and Development, *Measuring Health Care, 1960–1983: Expenditures, Costs and Performance, Social Policy Studies No. 2* (Paris: The Organization, 1985), p. 88.

Table 11: Staff per Bed, Exclusive of Physicians, 1960 and 1983, and Percentage of Increase

	1960		1983		Percentage of Increase
United Kingdom	NA		NA		NA
Sweden	0.71		1.74	(1982)	145
Canada	1.38		2.13	(1982)	54
West Germany	0.80	(1970)	1.14	(1982)	42
France	0.75	(1970)	1.37		83
Australia	NA		3.27	(1980)	NA
United States	0.96		2.69	(1981)	182

Source: Organization for Economic Cooperation and Development, *Measuring Health Care, 1960–1983: Expenditures, Costs and Performance*, Social Policy Studies No. 2 (Paris: The Organization, 1985), p. 115.

Table 12: Physician Consultations per Person per Year, 1960 and 1983

	1960		1983	
United Kingdom	3.8	(1972)	4.2	
Sweden	1.9	(1971)	2.7	
Canada	4.0	(1962)	5.5	(1981)
West Germany	NA		NA	
France	2.9	(1963)	4.7	(1983)
Australia	4.4	(1970)	6.4	(1981)
United States	4.5	(1963)	4.6	(1981)

Source: Organization for Economic Cooperation and Development, *Measuring Health Care, 1960–1983: Expenditures, Costs and Performance*, Social Policy Studies No. 2 (Paris: The Organization, 1985), p. 85.

number of beds is a factor, and it will be recalled that Sweden has no gatekeeper general practitioner. It is of interest to compare the United Kingdom and the United States for both 1960 and the early 1980s. Outpatient consultations with physicians are free in the United Kingdom, and in both 1960 and 1981 out-of-hospital consultations in the United States were by and large not free at time of service, yet consultations in the United States exceed those in the United Kingdom.

Although the data are quite fragmentary and will not be presented in a table, the number of dental visits per person is of interest because of the inherent potential for prevention of disease and for monitoring teeth through life.[5] Among the four countries with data (the United Kingdom, Sweden, West Germany, and the United States), the United States had by far the highest number of dental visits per person, 1.7 per year, and Sweden the lowest, 0.4 per year. Australia had 1.3 dental visits per year, the United

Kingdom 0.6 visits per year, and West Germany 0.5 visits per year. The United States, with no free dental services to speak of, has the highest visit ratio in the world; the United Kingdom and Sweden, with free dental services, have about one-third the rate of the United States. These data must reveal something about a nation's concept of dental health.

Variations of hospital admission rates are shown in Table 13. Except for Canada, admission rates have increased since the 1960s. The increases in France and Australia, in particular, stand out. The right-hand column shows that the differences in rates are considerable; for example, 21 percent for Australia and 12.7 percent for the United Kingdom.

In Table 14, hospital bed days per person per year, Sweden stands out both in 1960 and 1983, with 4.3 days and 4.8 days, respectively. In fact, Sweden's number of bed days per person is the highest of the countries covered (as well as of those not covered). It will be recalled that Sweden also had comparatively high bed-to-population ratios.

As reported in Table 15, the average length of stay decreased in all countries between 1960 and the early 1980s. These data are somewhat distorted by the inclusion of psychiatric hospitals, which have longer lengths of stay, but psychiatric hospitals have shortened their length of stay as well.

Table 16 shows the average number of cases treated per nonpsychiatric hospital bed per year. Since the average length of stay has become shorter, it follows of course that the patient turnover would be greater. All countries have increased the number of patients treated per bed per year, which presumably means that the hospitals (and physicians) are more efficient. In the early 1980s Sweden had the lowest turnover rate, with 16 cases per bed per year, and the United States, with 35 per year, had the highest. The European and British hospitals are assumed to have a comparatively large proportion of elderly, long-term patients because of a smaller supply of nursing homes, thus reducing comparability with the United States. Obviously, these statistics are quite "woolly" and difficult to interpret.

The data on surgical procedures, on consumption of pharmaceutical products, and on patterns of treatment of end-stage renal failure are not easy to interpret either. Table 17 presents rates of selected, relatively common surgical procedures. For coronary bypass for males around 1980, Sweden had the lowest rate with 25 procedures per 100,000 population, and the United States the highest with 99, comparing the four countries for which data are given. But the United States had the lowest appendectomy rate, 134 procedures per 100,000 population, and Australia the highest, 286; Canada had the highest cholecystectomy rate, 120 procedures per 100,000 population, and Australia the lowest, 74. Adding to the seeming confusion, Sweden and the United Kingdom had the lowest prostatectomy rates, 70 procedures per 100,000 population, and the United States the highest at 308.

Table 13: Hospital Admission Rates as Percentage of Total Population, 1960 and 1983

	1960		1983	
United Kingdom	9.2		12.7	(1981)
Sweden	13.4		19.2	
Canada	15.0		14.7	(1982)
West Germany	12.5		18.1	(1982)
France	6.7	(1966)	11.8	
Australia	12.5	(1961)	21.0	(1980)
United States	13.9		17.0	(1981)

Source: Organization for Economic Cooperation and Development, *Measuring Health Care, 1960–1983: Expenditures, Costs and Performance*, Social Policy Studies No. 2 (Paris: The Organization, 1985), p. 83.

Table 14: Hospital Bed Days per Person per Year, 1960 and 1983

	1960		1983	
United Kingdom	3.4		2.4	(1981)
Sweden	4.3		4.8	
Canada	1.8		2.1	(1982)
West Germany	3.6		3.4	(1982)
France	2.6		3.1	
Australia	2.4	(1963)	3.2	(1981)
United States	2.8		1.7	(1981)

Source: Organization for Economic Cooperation and Development, *Measuring Health Care, 1960–1983: Expenditures, Costs and Performance*, Social Policy Studies No. 2 (Paris: The Organization, 1985), p. 82.

Table 15: Average Length of Stay in All Hospitals, 1960 and 1983

	1960		1983	
United Kingdom	35.9		18.6	(1981)
Sweden	31.8		22.7	
Canada	11.1		13.3	(1982)
West Germany	28.7		18.7	(1982)
France	22.8	(1961)	14.1	
Australia	9.8	(1967)	7.4	(1980)
United States	20.5		9.9	(1981)

Source: Organization for Economic Cooperation and Development, *Measuring Health Care, 1960–1983: Expenditures, Costs and Performance*, Social Policy Studies No. 2 (Paris: The Organization, 1985), p. 84.

Table 16: Cases Treated per Nonpsychiatric Hospital Bed per Year, 1960 and 1983

	1960		1983	
United Kingdom	15		27	
Sweden	14		16	(1982)
Canada	21		22	(1981)
West Germany	16	(1970)	19	(1982)
France	13		21	(1980)
Australia	24	(1965)	33	(1981)
United States	32		35	(1980)

Source: Organization for Economic Cooperation and Development, *Measuring Health Care, 1960–1983: Expenditures, Costs and Performance*, Social Policy Studies No. 2 (Paris: The Organization, 1985), p. 115.

The surgical rates for females also show wide ranges. Take hysterectomies, for example. Medical indications for hysterectomies are rather controversial in practice, as revealed in the wide variations in hysterectomy rates. The United States has the highest number of hysterectomies per 100,000 population, 556, and the United Kingdom the lowest, 132. Sweden is also relatively low, 145, and Canada and Australia are relatively high, 470 and 405, respectively. Further perusal of the table will show additional anomalies that cry for explanation.

Successful treatment for end-stage renal failure is relatively new in the medical armamentarium; it appeared as clinically feasible around 1970 and created a whole new "market." Table 18 shows the enormous increase in patients receiving end-stage treatment—dialysis, kidney grafts, or both—per 1,000,000 population in the study countries. The United States leads by far with 306, and the United Kingdom is the lowest with 153. The United States is the only country that funds dialysis and grafts on demand, given medical indications. A reasonable inference would be that countries with lower rates, particularly the United Kingdom, must be letting patients die because of strict medical specifications to justify treatment, given other high priorities and a tight budget.[6]

The utilization data end with the consideration of pharmaceuticals, another form of treatment revealing tremendous variations among countries and undoubtedly reflecting great variations in professional judgment and public demand. Table 19 shows trends in the average number of medicines consumed per person per year. I can only observe that these variations make no sense; see, for example, France with 28.9 medicines per year in 1981 and the United States with 4.3 in 1977. In any case, the consumption of pharmaceutical products is probably the most controversial issue in public programs and likely private ones as well.

Table 17: Surgical Procedures, per 100,000 Population by Sex, around 1980

	Males					Females			
	Coronary Bypass	Appendectomy	Hemorrhoidectomy	Cholecystectomy	Prostatectomy	Hysterectomy	Appendectomy	Hemorrhoidectomy	Cholecystectomy
United Kingdom	NA	NA	NA	NA	70	132	NA	NA	NA
Sweden	25	165	38	101	70	145	171	31	178
Canada	44	155	62	120	229	470	131	57	316
West Germany	NA	NA	NA	NA	NA	NA	NA	NA	NA
France	NA	NA	NA	NA	NA	NA	NA	NA	NA
Australia	52	286	113	74	183	405	394	85	216
United States	99	134	84	112	308	556	124	69	288

Source: Organization for Economic Cooperation and Development, *Measuring Health Care, 1960–1983: Expenditures, Costs and Performance, Social Policy Studies No. 2* (Paris: The Organization, 1985), p. 118.

Table 18: Patients Receiving Treatment for End-Stage Renal Failure per 1,000,000 Population, 1970 and 1983

	1970		1983
United Kingdom	23.0		153.1
Sweden	54.2		189.9
Canada	121.1	(1976)	273.8
West Germany	17.7		258.3
France	26.0		255.1
Australia	NA		NA
United States	76.0	(1974)	306.0

Source: Organization for Economic Cooperation and Development, *Measuring Health Care, 1960–1983: Expenditures, Costs and Performance*, Social Policy Studies No. 2 (Paris: The Organization, 1985), p. 119.

Table 19: Pharmaceutical Consumption per Person per Year, 1960 and 1983

	1960		1983	
United Kingdom	4.7		6.8	(1982)
Sweden	4.7	(1974)	4.6	
Canada	NA		NA	
West Germany	11.0	(1973)	NA	
France	21.3	(1974)	28.9	(1981)
Australia	3.0		7.5	(1981)
United States	4.7	(1964)	4.3	(1977)

Source: Organization for Economic Cooperation and Development, *Measuring Health Care, 1960–1983: Expenditures, Costs and Performance*, Social Policy Studies No. 2 (Paris: The Organization, 1985), p. 87.

Until there was political concern with rising expenditures, the foregoing data on supply and utilization were regarded as output indicators rather than input. All countries were moving toward the goal of increased access and use, a sociopolitical objective. When expenditures began to be regarded as input rather than output indicators, the standard measurements of health became the output indicators: mortality, length of life, and morbidity. The purpose of personal health services is to improve health. These conventional indicators, however, which were useful while the scourges of communicable diseases—airborne, waterborne, and infectious—were rampant and nutrition and housing were inadequate, are no longer relevant to the mortality and disease patterns of developed and industrialized countries. Preventing additional deaths is more and more difficult as more and more people survive past 70 years of age. (The segment of the population aged 85 or older is the fastest growing segment of old age groups.) Personal health services, as such, never did have much influence in lowering the death rates on an aggregate basis, as Thomas McKeown showed clearly in his book.[7] The death rates were lowered during the latter part of the nineteenth century and into the twentieth century by an improved environment for the human species. Immunization and inoculation were introduced after the communicable and infectious disease rates were already falling. At any rate, I selected standard mortality rates as the conventional indicators of health levels for the countries covered from 1950 to the 1980s, and I will explain why they are virtually worthless as output measures of personal health services in developed countries, or for that matter, in developing countries.

Data in Table 20 reveal the crude mortality rates by country between 1960 and 1983. During that period the rate increased for three countries and decreased for four. If the rates were standardized for the age composition of the population, it is likely that all countries would have shown a decrease in the mortality rate. The increase in the crude mortality rates for the United Kingdom, Sweden, and West Germany can be interpreted as a function of the populations of those countries aging faster than the populations of the other study countries. The populations of Canada, Australia, and the United States are younger. (The relative position of France cannot be explained without further investigation.) In any case, the crude mortality rate as a measure of the effect of personal health services is worthless.

Life expectancy at birth may come closer to measuring health levels, but, again, the relationship to personal health services is questionable. As illustrated in Table 21, life expectancy at birth lengthened during the 30 years between 1950 and 1980, especially for females. Females born in 1980 had a life expectancy ranging from 76 years in the United Kingdom to 79 years in Sweden and Canada; for males born in 1980, life expectancy ranged from 70 years in the United Kingdom, West Germany, France, and

Table 20: Crude Mortality Rates per 1,000 Population, 1960 and 1983

	1960	*1983*
United Kingdom	9.4	11.7
Sweden	10.0	10.9
Canada	7.7	7.0
West Germany	11.5	11.7
France	11.3	10.2
Australia	8.5	7.1
United States	9.4	8.5

Source: Organization for Economic Cooperation and Development, *Measuring Health Care, 1960–1983: Expenditures, Costs and Performance,* Social Policy Studies No. 2 (Paris: The Organization, 1985), p. 144.

the United States to 73 years in Sweden. Clearly the length of life has increased in all countries from 1950 to 1980. The causes of the increase have been multiple and difficult to disentangle, but personal health services (drawing on McKeown) must have had little to do with it.

The greatest faith is conventionally put in infant mortality and prenatal mortality rates as valid proxy indicators of the overall standard of living and health status of a country or area. The decrease in these rates over the last 30 years, not to mention the decrease during the 50 years before 1930, is remarkable, as shown in Table 22. The major reasons for the infant mortality rate decrease have been improvements in environmental factors—such things as cleanliness, improved nutrition, immunization, and general mothercraft. It seems reasonable to assume that the infant mortality rate is quite amenable to reduction by known general public health technology, improved environment, and mothercraft. The lower infant mortality rates get, however, the more genetic and biological factors come into play, requiring exceedingly sophisticated diagnostic and treatment procedures and yielding smaller and smaller improvements in results. In fact, there is now the possibility that by using these procedures to save infants we are increasing the number of infants with permanent chronic disabilities.

As a final observation on these selected indicators, I offer data on mortality from a condition clearly originating in lifestyle, cirrhosis of the liver caused by excessive alcohol consumption. Table 23 shows that, in all the study countries, the mortality rate from cirrhosis of the liver has increased since 1960, presumably associated with affluence. Around 1980 the rate of mortality from this disease among males was astonishing: from 5 per 100,000 males in the United Kingdom to 38 per 100,000 males in France, with West Germany close behind France, the rates in France and West Germany apparently reflecting wine and beer consumption, respectively. Although the Swedish rate is relatively low, Sweden now regards alcoholism as its number one public health problem since all the other indicators are comparatively low.

Summary

The conventional and available data on health services performance indicators have been presented in this chapter, and I stress the words conventional and available. Such as they are, it does not appear possible to relate them to the market-minimized/market-maximized continuum: there are too many other variables that need to be introduced. As a sociologist I must perforce mention cultural differences regarding lifestyles (wine and cirrhosis of the liver in France), medical practice styles (aggressive in the United States and conservative in the United Kingdom), the organizational

Table 21: Years of Life Expectancy at Birth by Sex, 1950 and 1980

	Females		Males	
	1950	*1980*	*1950*	*1980*
United Kingdom	71.3	75.9	66.5	70.2
Sweden	72.4	78.9	69.9	72.6
Canada	70.5	79.0	66.3	71.0
West Germany	68.3	76.5	64.4	69.7
France	69.7	78.3	63.9	70.1
Australia	71.7	78.0	66.5	70.9
United States	71.2	76.7	65.6	69.6

Source: Organization for Economic Cooperation and Development, *Measuring Health Care, 1960–1983: Expenditures, Costs and Performance*, Social Policy Studies No. 2 (Paris: The Organization, 1985), p. 131.

Table 22: Infant Mortality and Perinatal Mortality, 1950 and 1983

	Infant Mortality (percentage of live births during first year)		Perinatal Mortality (percentage of live births and stillbirths)		
	1950	*1983*	*1950*	*1983*	
United Kingdom	3.12	1.02	3.90	1.05	
Sweden	2.00	0.70	3.40	0.73	
Canada	3.70	0.85	3.60	1.02	(1982)
West Germany	5.53	1.03	4.99	0.96	(1982)
France	5.19	0.89	3.60	1.19	(1982)
Australia	2.52	0.96	3.60	1.22	
United States	2.92	1.09	3.25	1.26	(1981)

Source: Organization for Economic Cooperation and Development, *Measuring Health Care, 1960–1983: Expenditures, Costs and Performance*, Social Policy Studies No. 2 (Paris: The Organization, 1985), p. 131.

Table 23: Cirrhosis Mortality Trends per 100,000 Males, 1960 and 1982

	1960	*1982*		
United Kingdom	3.3	4.9		
Sweden	5.8	12.6	(17.0	1975)
Canada	7.9	13.0	(15.5	1980)
West Germany	24.7	34.4	(37.2	1981)
France	40.6	38.0		
Australia	6.0	11.8		
United States	15.3	17.9	(1980)	

Source: Organization for Economic Cooperation and Development, *Measuring Health Care, 1960–1983: Expenditures, Costs and Performance*, Social Policy Studies No. 2 (Paris: The Organization, 1985), p. 143.

structures through which health services are delivered, and the gatekeepers within the structures. All of these variables and more must somehow be incorporated in a research design for a fuller understanding of the differences among the health services systems of various countries and the relative openness of the economies in the continuum.

Economists delving into cross-national comparative expenditures have revealed, not surprisingly, using a sample of 21 developed countries, that national expenditure levels are related to per capita income.[8] The carefully crafted reports of the OECD reveal the methodological difficulties of generalizing from available data on the experiences of developed countries. These reports, like my book, produce a great deal of data, but we are not quite sure what to make of them. Even so, my inability to tease out generalizations from the performance indicators available may, in itself, be a contribution to the state of the art of cross-national comparative research, a major objective of this book. Obviously, a great deal of in-depth research for primary data—data not already collected for research purposes or not available at all—needs to be conducted. Research on internal institutional performance and household surveys on population behavior and attitudes need to be conducted to untangle this seeming confusion. Intuitively, it does not seem reasonable to conclude that these indicators are as random as they appear to be. Science in general has a faith that there is more order than meets the eye, even in the social sciences.

Notes

1. See Odin W. Anderson, "Toward an Understanding of the Health Services Enterprise" and "Incursions into Perceptions, Attitudes, and Decision Making," in *Health Services in the United States: A Growth Enterprise Since 1875* (Ann Arbor, MI: Health Administration Press, 1985), Chapters 18 and 19.
2. Organization for Economic Cooperation and Development, *Measuring Health Care, 1960–1983: Expenditures, Costs and Performance*, Social Policy Studies No. 2 (Paris: The Organization, 1985). The staff of OECD worked assiduously with relevant staffs in 24 countries to gather data. The prestige of OECD assured cooperation. The book reports the details of the methodology used, the problems of data supply, the problems of comparison, and explanations of the definitions. I, therefore, draw my operational and performance information from this report. This report was followed by a partial update in 1987, i.e., through 1985: Organization for Economic Cooperation and Development, *Financing and Delivering Health Care: A Comparative Analysis of OECD Countries*, Social Policy Studies No. 4 (Paris: The Organization, 1987). I certainly could not have carried out this kind of monumental effort myself. I made a modest attempt for three countries with fairly abundant data in my: *Health Care: Can There Be Equity? The United States, Sweden, and England* (New York: John Wiley & Sons, 1972). Another

attempt that received deserved recognition is: Robert J. Maxwell, *Health and Wealth: An International Study of Health-Care Spending* (Lexington, MA: Lexington Books, 1981). This was mainly a cross-sectional study of the middle 1970s and was limited to financial data. A recent book from which I drew historical and descriptive data is: Marshall W. Raffel, ed., *Comparative Systems: Descriptive Analyses of Fourteen National Health Systems* (University Park, PA: Pennsylvania State University Press, 1984). Statistical data were more or less available up to 1981.
3. Maxwell, *Health and Wealth.*
4. Joseph P. Newhouse, Geoffrey Anderson, and Leslie Roos, "Hospital Spending in the United States: A Comparison," *Health Affairs* 7 (Winter 1988): 6–16.
5. Organization for Economic Cooperation and Development, *Measuring Health Care, 1960–1983,* p. 86.
6. See Henry J. Aaron and William B. Schwartz, *The Painful Prescription: Rationing Hospital Care,* Studies in Social Economics (Washington, DC: Brookings Institution, 1984).
7. Thomas McKeown, *The Role of Medicine: Dream, Mirage, or Nemesis* (Princeton, NJ: Princeton University Press, 1979).
8. Organization for Economic Cooperation and Development, *Financing and Delivering Health Care,* p. 80.

Chapter 10

Responses to Rising Expenditures

Despite global fiscal controls in the form of budget caps, waiting lists for rationing of so-called elective surgery, and increases in payments at the time of service, none of the study countries is satisfied with the results of its efforts to slow the rise of health services expenditures. There are two major responses to escalating costs: attempts at overall planning and an increasing interest in having private practice and private insurance grow to siphon off some of the pressure on mainstream health insurance programs. These two responses seem contradictory although they both attempt to accomplish the same purpose—less costly and more efficient use of resources. On the one hand, social planning is motivated by equality of access, and on the other hand, private insurance is motivated by individual choice, which implies inequality based on ability to pay.

It is only in the last decade or so, even after years of universal health insurance, that countries have begun to take serious interest in overall strategic planning of their respective health services delivery systems. This comes as a surprise to Americans, who assume that countries that have universal health insurance engage in strategic planning as a matter of course. In fact, countries with universal health insurance have been as freewheeling in operating their health services delivery systems as has the United States. The major purpose of universal health insurance was to abolish the exchange of money between providers and patients at the time of service in order to remove the cost obstacle to access. This objective needed not planning but legislation, a type of legislation that has not been politically possible so far in the United States except for the elderly through Medicare, and now for the uninsured.

An important step toward equality of access in various liberal democracies was the enactment of universal health insurance. Later attention was paid to the proper distribution of services, so that resources would not be as unequally distributed as they were at the beginning of the universal health insurance. Very soon thereafter the accelerated increases in use, prices, and expenditures—particularly overall global expenditures—led to consideration of overall strategic planning to distribute services equitably and at the same time contain costs. Further, the rapid emergence of high-technology medicine led to problems of efficient distribution of medically dazzling, expensive, new resources.

A review of the techniques, styles, and results of planning in these countries reveals a great deal of frustration as to their effectiveness. The greatest complaint of the officially established planning agencies and planners is that they are hampered and their nicely laid plans are distorted by politicians who are too responsive to their constituents. Personnel in the planning agencies look at neat numbers and the general public interest; politicians look at people and their seemingly irrational desires.

The literature on actual planning and results in these countries is not copious for the health field. There is a fair amount of theoretical literature on the concept and techniques of health services planning.[1] There is also literature on social planning in general, notably by Braybrooke and Lindblom,[2] who subscribe empirically, as I do, to the incrementalist school of public policy formulation and implementation.

Theorists of this persuasion assert that overall social planning is impossible; they term such planning synoptic planning because there cannot possibly be enough information available. Even if there were adequate information available, policymakers would not know how to synthesize it for implementation. Planners and policymakers must select discrete problems at the margin because, as in the case of the health services, the systemic interrelationships are too numerous and volatile for directed and rational control. The Swedes have a term for this type of incremental planning process, *rullande prognose* or rolling prognosis. As Braybrooke and Lindblom put it, "While the incrementalist contemplates means, he continues at the same time to contemplate objectives, unlike the synoptic analyst who ideally must at some point finally stabilize his objective and then select the proper means."[3]

Planning

The United Kingdom may have tried harder than any other liberal democracy to plan the distribution of health services resources, based on epidemiological information. The major planning control is exerted through the central budget, which allocates differential amounts of money over time to the 14 regions, giving less to regions already relatively well supplied with hospital beds and more to regions not so well supplied. Also, the budget attempts to allocate less to hospitals and more to out-of-hospital services. The time allowed for completion of this apparently systematic plan is so long—about 20 years—that the plan is in effect incremental. The British, like the populations of liberal democracies generally, do not favor great and sudden changes in government.

Sweden has been regarded as a model for systematic planning based on data gathering, with the regionalization of the tertiary hospitals being cited as an example. As described in Chapter 4, Sweden was ripe for this kind of regionalization because the major medical centers were already in place through the incremental logic of the Swedish health services development. It will be recalled that the bulk of the Swedish health services is owned, funded, and operated by the counties. In 1983, the new government law was gradually (or not so gradually) turning the entire administrative and financial responsibility for both inpatient and outpatient services to the counties, where it would be close to the people. The government does not tell the counties how to organize the services, but access to the full spectrum of services must be provided in one way or another.

The frustrations inherent in other liberal democracies' efforts at planning can be inferred from the considered remarks of experts from these countries. While some of the statements reported here date back to the mid-1970s, the intervening decade did not change the situation to any marked degree.

At a conference in 1976, John McLeod of Toronto, Canada, observed, "Canadians have learned that unless a start is made quickly, even with adequate planning, one could wait forever for the ideal system and for all the answers. It is experience, not technology, that will help formulate the questions, and it is the trial and error of experience that will most likely produce the answers. The icy water will not warm up; one has to take the plunge."[4] This remark was directed, in McLeod's view, to the American obsession with marshaling facts before taking action on universal health insurance, which Canada inaugurated largely on faith. Still, surprisingly, he did not feel Canadian health insurance had solved the basic problems of personal health services because neither morbidity nor mortality rates had been significantly lowered. "We have paid for access to an imperfect system."

At another international meeting, another Canadian, an authority on the history of health services policy in Canada remarked, "Then [in 1949] we had the necessary information [on hospitals and their use in Saskatchewan]. We knew where every patient went, who the hospital clientele was, and its trading area. We developed an ideal master plan. But 20 years later we have a surplus of hospitals and we have reduced the size of others. One wonders what went wrong with the planning."[5]

Finally, I draw from another Canadian (appropriately, Americans are closely watching their next-door neighbor). Robert Evans, an academic economist who facetiously observes, "So we have achieved in the early 1970s an unsatisfactory health care system with which most Canadians are satisfied."[6] This was an astute observation of dissatisfied experts but a satisfied public.

Christa Altenstetter of West Germany observed, "The reconciliation of diverse constituent units within a federal system that needs rational planning is almost an impossible task. In line with organizational diversity due to different *Länd* [state] constitutions, *Länd* administrations, policy preference, and implementing capabilities, the institutional process by which plans are developed, the participants in the process, and the agreed upon goals vary greatly from *Länd* to *Länd*."[7]

In his memoirs, the former director general of the Swedish board of health, Arthur Engel, reminisced with some pride, "Immediately after being taken over by the County Councils [1862], the Swedish hospital system entered into a development phase that has made our hospitals famous. As I see it this happened because the responsibility for the revolution was placed with a self-governing, locally elected body which knew the needs and understood the psychology of the population."[8] Engel did not, however, draw the implication that if local areas are given the choice, they place a high priority on health services even if the cost is directly visible in local taxes. Sweden emerged with the highest bed-to-population ratio in the liberal-democratic countries and now regards itself as overbedded.

Robert Bridgman of France, speaking on planning in Europe, listed ten obstacles to strategic planning. They included the familiar ones of vested interests, physician opposition, and the variety of hospital ownership that gives the government little leverage. He seemed to wish that France could have started with a clean slate. He observed that in evaluating the progress of hospital regionalization in European countries, it was found that nowhere was regionalization fully implemented. He admired the seeming ability of the socialist countries to regionalize hospitals, but he also feared that the strictly ordered hierarchical structure of implementation resulted in certain rigidities and significant delays.[9]

Erik Holst, a professor of social medicine in Denmark, reported that in Denmark in 1976 there was one "unholy alliance" between general practitioners and the public negotiators. The practitioners wanted the number of those allowed to practice in a given area strictly controlled. The public negotiators realized that additional general practitioners could mean better primary care but that their services in total would cost more money. The negotiators sided with the practitioners. Holst further observed that the emphasis shifted from empirical health to tax reduction. He then wondered if it would not be better to have pluralism in funding services rather than a financial system totally dependent on taxes.[10]

This review of quotations from health care experts and authorities can well be concluded with observations on the British National Health Service as recorded in the report of the Royal Commission on the National Health Service on the management of finances in the service. They show how difficult planning can be.

> These decisions [in the NHS budget] are the outcome of political judgments on the total size and distribution of public expenditure in the light of assessment of the financial and economic outlook under the Government's social and other problems.[11]
>
> Because there is no output clearly measurable in money terms, and affecting the results of the years' operation, it requires special efforts to pursue efficiency and effectiveness with the vigor with which expenditure itself is controlled.[12]
>
> Many of the staff whom we spoke to in NHS [including members of the planning teams] wanted certainty over future resources. The DHSS made it clear that this cannot be guaranteed and that planning must consider uncertainty directly.[13]
>
> Generally the NHS staff we spoke to did not understand the link between central and local planning and control. . . . When the relationships between central decisions and their eventual local effects are not understood, it is not surprising that changes made centrally are not viewed sympathetically when they cause local difficulties. In such cases staff argue there is little point in attempting to introduce rational methods into local decision making about resources, given that they have to act in what seems to be an irrational way to meet central demands and controls.[14]
>
> The planning process, however imperfectly developed it may be in the very early years following the reorganization of the health services, consists essentially of an administrative process of exchanges of priorities, proposals, reviews, arguments, and counter-arguments, downwards and upwards through the tiers of the NHS.[15]
>
> Decisions in capital budgeting rely on professional judgment and not on formal criteria for the evaluation of capital developments. We see little early prospect of defining satisfactory measures to make this process more scientific, so that allocation has still to involve subjective choice by accountable management teams.[16]

In the context of another international meeting, Sir George Godber, former chief medical officer of the British National Health Service candidly remarked, "Perhaps we, in Great Britain, have kept down the expenditures too much, but we managed by methods of consultations, both locally and centrally, to try and prevent the technologists from running away with everything."[17]

An appropriate climax to this litany of problems in planning is an observation made by the commission staff that there was constant danger of "allocation by decibel."[18]

A few years after the report of the Royal Commission on the National Health Service, Christopher Ham, a political sociologist, wrote

> What the impact on priority services [mental health, out of hospital services, chronic illness] will be is still unclear, although there is certainly the possibility of non-conformity to national policies and perhaps inertia as national guidelines are interpreted by health authorities [in regional districts]. However, such a possibility already exists, and it may be that a series of locally based incremental changes will be more effective in producing the kinds of shifts in resource allocation that the originally centrally guided planning systems sought to bring out.[19]

Lurking behind these observations is a realization that trying to direct the future of health services is really an incremental process. Policymakers and planners wish it were not so. Coming to terms with this realization is regarded as a compromise which is compromising rather than as a process leading to an equilibrium of resources, financing, public expectation and political pressure groups. The Nordic countries appear to be aware of this, as is illustrated in a joint report for the World Health Organization on the status of planning in Norway, Sweden, Iceland, Denmark, and Finland.[20] Representatives from the health services in each country assemble annually to present papers on their common problems. These Nordic countries share a common culture of health services' being a public responsibility, of local autonomy with central guidance, and of an egalitarian philosophy suffusing their moral values. Hence the articles in their report reflect a narrow range of consensus much more difficult to attain in more heterogeneous societies on the Continent and in North America. The result is a pragmatic, common-sense view of problem solving.

Victor Rodwin examined the planning processes in France, the province of Quebec, England, and the United States and concluded that none of them is effective, because none of these countries gives planners and planning agencies control over financing.[21] (The federal institutions on planning in the United States set up in 1975 have been abandoned.) This situation seems to be general among developed, liberal-democratic countries. It seems reasonable that it might well be a political decision not to give a government agency that much combined power beyond that of the elected legislative body.

Two international workshops on planning, the first in Copenhagen in 1977 and the second in New Orleans in 1978, were a joint project of the U.S. Department of Health, Education, and Welfare, the Health Resources Administration, the Bureau of Health Planning, and the Pan American Health Organization/World Health Organization. Twenty-six countries participated. The objective of the project was "to improve health planning at the local and regional level in the United States with the concomitant effect of improving health planning generally throughout the world." The two workshops were held to facilitate the exchange of information on health planning. Henrik Blum prepared a report synthesizing the problems, techniques, methods, and processes of planning.[22] It was a sophisticated tour de force on the art and politics of planning in showing that planning methodologies must be cognizant of political styles and pressure groups and the desires of the public. Planning cannot be a purely technocratic exercise. Given the data, the statistical techniques are quite self-evident. The report set out in great detail what must be considered in various circumstances, of which there are as many as there are countries. Hence there can be no planning model, but only planners exceedingly sensitized as to how to proceed.

The spectrum of the dominant social, economic, and political ideologies must be taken into account and respected. The particular ideology determines, in the main, a country's posture on:

(1) the desirability of undertaking deliberate social change, i.e., the use of planning in and from the public sphere, and (2) if desirable, by what kinds of interests and by what kinds of planning approaches.

The report continues:

The spectrum of SEP ideologies runs from a perception that public government exists specifically to plan for and attain whatever it thinks is good for its people to a belief that absolutely no government action is justified other than to maintain an environment in which private enterprise can privately plan, organize, and produce whatever and however it wishes.[23]

The obvious polar social, economic, political systems pointed out were the United States and the Union of Soviet Socialist Republics. The report goes on, "What emerges is that different SEP ideologies allow for different planning approaches which in turn essentially tolerate only certain structures, processes, and participants. These in turn pretty much dictate the choice of methodologies or at least determine which are likely to produce products which can be tolerated or utilized in each setting."[24] The paradox, however, is that

for planning to be acceptable it must live within the bounds set up by its social determinants; but to be successful and get support, it not only has to be acceptable, but must be able to overcome the very problems which are in great part the inevitable outcomes of the same set of societal determinants which created the planning machinery, and probably set it up so that it cannot attack the problems.[25]

The report cautions against "the blind collection of data," although it considers it important that an information system be designed to cover the entire range of concerns of health. In other words, the complete system must be envisioned—no easy task given the extreme complexity of the elements to be planned. If consensus is to be a major force in planning, there are further complications, hence the incremental approach rather than the synoptic. The whole system is too difficult to grasp.

A recent article by Albert van der Werff in essence elaborates on Blum's observation, but being an economist, van der Werff believes that the major problem in the planning and management of health services is the lack of financial incentives to make providers be cost conscious and avoid procedures and services at the margin of usefulness. Planning in itself does not, in his view, remove this defect.[26] He does not fully face, however, the inherent difficulty of applying the economist's concept of efficiency to personal health services, of how to relate input and output.

Nevertheless, van der Werff's is a brilliant article because it takes the rare step of posing the problems realistically. In summary, the point of view developed is that there is no single solution that is best under all circumstances.

> The conclusion is that the selection of a particular theory or method of planning and management should depend both on the objectives of the decision maker and on the determinants of the planning environment. General prescriptions should not be made. At the same time, some elements have to be stressed in all types of planning, namely: the orientation towards outcomes or outputs of problems; the attention to long-term strategic thinking; and, the application of some efficient, flexible and less bureaucratic approaches.[27]

This would appear to be a tall order; he is requesting an art, not a technical-model methodology.

Planning is like the experience of a motorist who is driving on a narrow, dangerous, and winding mountain road in the rain. He chances to meet a car at a mud puddle. On passing the other car, the motorist driving up the mountain has his windshield splashed with muddy water. He turns on his windshield wiper but it does not work. Being innovative, he adjusts his rearview mirror so that he can see backward as far as possible. He thereupon extrapolates where the road ahead is by watching the curves in the road behind. The moral, of course, is that this is the state of the art of planning in the health services.

While the United Kingdom has tended toward synoptic-incremental planning, the United States is currently resorting to corporate planning. The big hospital–medical centers (megacenters) have planning and development units to analyze the service environment relative to other centers trying to establish their "turfs," to determine the appropriate economy of scale, and, where they nudge each other, to work out cooperative arrangements to share high technology, and, if this is not feasible, to compete directly in a trucelike atmosphere.

What Is the Private Sector?

All countries that have universal health insurance also have private health services, no matter how small—a fact indicative of the inherent correlation between the developed physician-patient relationship and personal health. The developed countries in the liberal-democratic orbit created a market-oriented economy and a political parliamentary system that sanction this type of economy and facilitate private health services. Such an economy tries to minimize government interference in the operation of the means of production and distribution, that is, in the daily lives of people making a living. Later in the nineteenth and twentieth centuries, government-sponsored and -operated programs emerged to mitigate "the slings and arrows of outrageous fortune" caused by unemployment, severance from the labor market because of age or disability, and the increasing expense of personal health services which often threatens family financial solvency. In the liberal-democratic political context, these developments are known as welfare-state capitalism.

It seems that before personal health services became expensive, resulting in high-cost episodes of illness, they were regarded as more or less personal problems. Exceptions were the need for mental hospitals and for care for patients with long-term illnesses such as tuberculosis. As noted in the descriptions of the countries selected, in the early days within the free enterprise framework, the mitigation of the financial effects of sickness, absenteeism, and the costs of physician and general hospital services was found in voluntary associations of workers, called benefit associations, and private philanthropy. Tax support for the care of the very poor and the working poor, emerged very slowly.

The emphasis was on voluntary self-help by private means. Gradually, the voluntary and philanthropic resources proved to be insufficient, giving way to government-sponsored health insurance for one group of the population after another. In the liberal-democratic context, countries can be ranged as to the nature and composition of the mix between private and public financing, ownership, and reimbursement methods. Voluntary health associations persisted outside of the government health insurance mainstream for particular diseases and for support for research. Volunteer work in hospitals to offer amenities such as books, flowers, and extra receptionist help might also be mentioned. As the egalitarian philosophy was more and more adopted in practice, government became the major social and political vehicle to implement that philosophy. In some countries, the government negotiated with private hospitals for services for the mandated population. In other countries, like Sweden, there were hardly any private hospitals; the hospitals were, and are, owned by the county councils. In the United Kingdom, the government expropriated the hospitals. Still, an appreciable number of beds there remain privately owned. In 1983, in England, 6 percent of the acute care beds were in private hospitals, and they were increasing in number.[28] (Some 2 percent to 3 percent of the beds in National Health Service hospitals are pay beds, but over the years the pay beds have been reduced in number.)

Remnants of privatism in the liberal-democratic countries are seen in the persistence of freestanding physicians who contract for services with the various governments as independent entrepreneurs or under fee-for-service and capitation methods of payments. Further, what is emerging as a pattern of private insurance coverage, notably in the United Kingdom and Scandinavia and undoubtedly in other countries with universal health insurance (although solid data are scarce; there are only anecdotes and reasonable inferences), is that of private insurance bought by employers for their employees or directly by individuals to avoid the long waiting lists for elective surgery that can be delayed without damage to health, to assure free choice of a specialist where patients may self-refer, and for private beds in hospitals.

In 1986 in England and Wales, for example, 13.2 percent of all elective surgery was performed in private hospitals and in private-pay beds in National Health Service hospitals (9.8 percent in private hospitals and 3.4 percent in private-pay beds).[29] Of hemorrhoidectomies, hip replacements, hysterectomies, and varicose vein repairs, 27.2 percent, 26.2 percent, 20.9 percent, and 23.0 percent, respectively, were performed in private hospitals and National Health Service private-pay beds. It is obvious that these conditions are not generally lethal and that they can be delayed.

There was a great deal of political excitement in Sweden and Norway in 1986 over the appearance of private clinics, established by physicians from private capital, that cater to uncomfortable but nonlethal conditions.[30] These clinics charge fees and are very well equipped, with pleasant reception and consultation rooms.

The public systems have been caught with a backlog of hip replacements, cataract operations, lens replacements, and even artery-bypass surgery, because the technology for them was perfected so quickly. All of a sudden, new technology created new needs and demands, and the public systems could not respond quickly enough because of slow decision making and difficulty in raising capital.

The ideological supporters of government health insurance fear that tax support for the public sector will be eroded. Governments are reeling under the impact of accelerating health care costs and, while private clinics and private insurance may relieve the pressure on the public treasury, there is at the same time a possibility that their availability will increase public resistance to the progressive income tax. Still, however, the public insurance systems are so well entrenched in the social fabric of all the countries (except, of course, the United States and possibly Australia) that private clinics and private insurance do not appear to be a threat to the public systems unless the latter become grossly underfunded. The founder and director of the Ring Clinic in Oslo is on record as saying that he supports the public system, but in a liberal democracy people should also have a choice of health services alternatives if they feel that the public system is too inconvenient. The clinic has built its own, posh, 150-bed hospital on the outskirts of Oslo.[31]

It seems that the issue of the private sector's being a threat to the egalitarian value of equal access to health services is more pronounced in the United Kingdom and the Scandinavian countries than on the Continent, where the health services are quite pluralistic. This is not to say that the Continental countries do not have a deep sense of social solidarity but that they seem to be less puristic than their neighbors in what egalitarian means. In the United Kingdom and Scandinavia the discussions and debates take on an either-or character as if no equitable compromise were possible. If the private sector continues to grow, it is likely that the debates will assume a greater sophistication about the proper place of private clinics for health services in a liberal democracy.[32]

The varying relationships of existing private health insurance to the public health insurance programs can, it seems, be classified as follows:

1. Private health insurance can be a supplement to rather than a substitute for the mainstream government insurance, providing amenities: private rooms, convenience of access for elective services, and direct access to specialists without first going through a general practitioner as the gatekeeper, as is done in England. The small private health insurance sector is a safety valve for what can be called the pressure cooker of feeling about the National Health Service.

2. Private health insurance can be a clear alternative in direct competition with the mainstream government health insurance, the latter insurance becoming one of the alternatives. Australia approaches this method.

3. Private health insurance can be the main vehicle to underwrite and administer a universal health insurance scheme for the government, with regulations. West Germany approaches this concept.

4. Private health insurance through employers can be the main vehicle for the bulk of the employed population, with the government

picking up segments that private health insurance is inherently incapable of covering or not expected to cover. The obvious existing example is the United States.

5. Private health insurance can be used to cover services uninsured by the mainstream government health insurance. This is characteristic of Canada.

There may be other variants, but the foregoing are the main ones.

Turning back to the United Kingdom, the Nuffield Provincial Hospital Trust, a private foundation devoted to health services concerns, and the National Health Service sponsored a series of essays to examine the implications of the search for "supplementary financial provision alongside taxation."[33] Given the entrenched position that the National Health Service continues to enjoy, the sponsoring of these essays signified the seriousness with which its original mission and the costs necessary to continue to fulfill this mission are regarded. The Trust, in addition, sought experts from Great Britain, Canada, the Netherlands, Belgium, the Federal Republic of Germany, France, Australia, and the United States for their perspectives regarding the nature of the public-private mix.

The experts endeavored to describe the public-private mix, the implications of varying the relative proportions of this mix for cost control and equity, and the possibilities for change. Each observer was frustrated in envisioning how change could take place in each system. Health services systems in all countries are notoriously hard to change. They are intertwined with the interests of providers, the citizenry, special disease groups, the sources of funding, and the methods and amounts of reimbursement. All countries are afraid of too much change because they are not too discontent with the present systems. Existing systems are familiar. They operate tolerably well, but they could do a better job: they could be less costly, more equitable, better distributed, and so on. Overall, however, there is a feeling that the systems are out of control. British observers of national health services cannot extricate themselves from the awesome edifice of the National Health Service, nor is it even practical for them to do so. American observers are unable to transcend the current fluid U.S. health services scene but have to roll with the swirl of forces, which is about all that can be done under the circumstances. Canadian observers believe that privatization should build on the present provincial-federal structure. No one envisions a quick fix. Whatever degree of privatization is indicated, it should not be carried so far as to drain resources away from mainstream government health insurance or health service system. In fact the editors of the volume of British essays, *The Public/Private Mix for Health*, generalize that "if the mix is altered, one set of policy problems is likely to be exchanged for another."[34] In their concluding and overview chapter, Gordon McLachlan and

Alan Maynard come to a ringing conclusion precluding much change: "After receiving the evidence we have accumulated over these past few months, as well as from our own collective experience and observation, we both feel that despite its faults, the variety of complex services which is termed the National Health Service constitutes a unique and precious proportion of the GDP compared to other countries."[35] Extreme ideological positions toward either the market-minimized or market-maximized end of the health services continuum are reviewed as utopian. This implies that current health delivery systems embody the best of all possible worlds so far but should be improved on the margin.

The future growth of the private sector relative to the public sector is not easy to predict. If the public health insurance programs continue to threaten to slow down and if tighter budgets for an inherently dynamic enterprise result in rationing, waiting lists, and other inconveniences, the private sector will grow. A modified, politically acceptable concept of equity will have to be formulated. An egalitarian concept was easy to implement in a period of economic expansion after World War II, but not so in a period of slower growth and possibly no growth at all. A sufficiently large residual of affluent people will opt out for convenience and choice.

The placement in the continuum of the relationships between the private and public sectors will remain problematic as long as the private sector is not forbidden altogether—an unlikely eventuality in the liberal democracies where the private sector has such a strong tradition in the ownership and production of goods and services including the personal health services. Although in the main I do not believe personal health services are a commodity in the pure market sense of the concept, it would seem that these services have in common with a commodity that aspect which lends itself to choices—in this case, choices that do not threaten life, such as convenience of elective surgery and choice of specialist.

Options for health insurance will remain strong in the continuum, starting with the countries on the Continent and continuing through Australia and the United States. Not only will they remain strong, but the options themselves will be diversified. In the continuum from the United Kingdom through Canada, private insurance will continue to exist as an option, but grudgingly so. No government is able to provide all of the choices that people want from a bundle of services as complex as personal health services.

On a bolder note, I predict that if the United States finally attains a universal health service under which no one is uninsured, it is likely that a large minority of the more affluent Americans, possibly 40 percent, will buy private insurance to supplement their regular coverage and that some will opt out altogether (in luxury HMOs, for example) or play the entire system.

The United States is exceedingly reluctant to raise taxes for equity and universal health insurance sufficient to provide a middle- or upper-middle-class service for all. The United Kingdom has demonstrated this trait as well, but the British population is much less demanding.

Notes

1. Henrik L. Blum, *Planning for Health: Developments and Application of Social Change Theory* (New York: Human Sciences Press, 1974).
2. David Braybrooke and Charles E. Lindblom, *A Strategy of Decision: Policy Evaluation as a Social Process* (New York: Free Press, 1970).
3. Ibid., p. 133.
4. John P. McLeod, "Canadian Experience with Health Manpower Planning," in *Changing National Sub-National Relations in Health: Opportunities and Constraints,* ed. Christa Altenstetter. Proceedings of an International Conference, Bethesda, MD, May 24–26, 1976. U.S. Department of Health, Education and Welfare Publication No. (NIH) 78–128 (Washington, DC: Government Printing Office, 1978), p. 45.
5. Malcolm Taylor, during discussion, in *Policies for the Containment of Health Care Costs and Expenditures,* ed. Stuart O. Schweitzer. Proceedings of a Conference, Bethesda, MD, April 26–28, 1976. U.S. Department of Health, Education and Welfare Publication No. (NIH) 78–184 (Washington, DC: Government Printing Office, 1978), p. 431.
6. Robert G. Evans, "Health Costs and Expenditures in Canada," in *International Health Costs and Expenditures,* ed. Teh-wei Hu. Proceedings of an International Conference, Bethesda, MD, June 2–4, 1975. U.S. Department of Health, Education and Welfare Publication No. (NIH) 76–1067 (Washington, DC: Government Printing Office, 1976), p. 63.
7. Altenstetter, ed., *Changing National Sub-National Relations,* note 4, p. 223.
8. Arthur Engel, *Perspectives in Health Planning* (London: Athlone Press, 1968), p. 70.
9. Robert Bridgman, "Hospital Regionalization in Europe: Achievements and Obstacles," in *Changing National Sub-National Relations,* ed. Altenstetter, pp. 325–29.
10. Erik Holst, World Medical Association, Follow-up Committee on Development and Allocation of Medical Care Resources, July 30–August 1, 1979 (Tokyo: The Association, n.d.), p. 161.
11. Royal Commission on the National Health Service, *Management of Financial Resources in the National Health Services,* Research Paper No. 2 (London: Her Majesty's Stationery Office, 1978), p. 17.
12. Ibid., p. 21.
13. Ibid., p. 24.
14. Ibid., p. 27.
15. Ibid., p. 82.
16. Ibid., p. 84.
17. U.S. Department of Health, Education and Welfare, *The Doctor-Patient Relationship in the Changing Health Scene.* Proceedings of an International Con-

ference, Bethesda, MD, April 26–28, 1976. DHEW Publication No. (NIH) 78–183 (Washington, DC: Government Printing Office, 1978), p. 366.
18. Royal Commission on the National Health Service, *Management of Financial Resources,* p. 95.
19. Christopher Ham, *Health Policy in Britain: The Politics and Organization of the National Health Service* (London: Macmillan Press, 1982), p. 56.
20. Nordiska Ministerrådets Sekretarariat I Oslo, *Halso-och Sjukvårds Planering I Norden (Health Care Planning in the North)* (Oslo: Nordic Council of Ministers Secretariat, NU A1978: 13).
21. Victor G. Rodwin, *The Health Planning Predicament: France, Quebec, England, and the United States* (Berkeley: University of California Press, 1984), Chapter 1.
22. Henrik L. Blum, *Health Planning Methods: An International Perspective. Report of the 1978 International Workshop.* U.S. Department of Health, Education and Welfare Publication No. (H12A) 79–14042 (Washington, DC: Government Printing Office, September 1979).
23. Ibid., p. 15.
24. Ibid., p. 20.
25. Ibid., p. 29.
26. Albert van der Werff, "Planning and Management for Health in Periods of Economic Stringency and Instability: A Contingency Approach," *International Journal of Health Planning and Management* 1 (1986): 227–40.
27. Ibid., p. 227.
28. Grant Thornton Management Consultants, *Health Services Management: Competition and Cooperation, A Way to Improve Health Sector Performance.* A Report. (London: Nuffield Provincial Hospital Trust, 1986), p. 40.
29. Ibid., p. 42.
30. Lilly Kristiansen, "Jeg ser!" *Ring Journalen* 2, No. 2 (1986). The title means "I see" and was published by the Ring Medical Center in Oslo which I visited.
31. "Ring Medisinske Senter-En Helsepolitisk Brannfakkel," interview with Jens Moe, *Tidsskrift for Norsk Legeforening* 105 (1985): 988–90. (Translation: The Ring Medical Center, A Health Politics Torch.)
32. The following references illustrate what I mean: United Kingdom: Michael Lee, *Private and National Health Services* (London: Policy Studies Institute, Vol. XLIV, No. 578, July 1978); Sweden: Egon Jonsson and Douglas Skalin, eds., *Privat och Offentlig Sjukvård, Samverkan eller Konkurrens* (Stockholm: SPRI, 1985); Norway: Håkon Lorentzen, *Privat eller Offentlig Velferd?* (Oslo: Oslo University Press, 1984).
33. Gordon McLachlan and Alan Maynard, eds., *The Public/Private Mix for Health: The Relevance and Effects of Change* (London: Nuffield Provincial Hospital Trust, 1982), pp. 1, 2.
34. Ibid., p. 21.
35. Ibid., p. 555.

Chapter 11

Observations and Conclusions

The overwhelming impression one gets from a review of the evolution of seven countries' personal health services delivery systems and their expenditure and use patterns is of the operation of powerful and seemingly uncontrollable forces that have driven and shaped this complex service institution since the last quarter of the nineteenth century. No central or local authorities, public or private, set forth a blueprint of how to direct and shape the evolution of the delivery systems. They were an integral part of the evolution of the economic and political systems themselves, an evolution of growth and expansion: more goods, more services, more voters as the franchise expanded to the entire adult population. Economic growth yielded social surpluses for health services, social insurances, and a higher standard of living. As their economies grew, the countries were able to devote more and more resources to "unproductive" but humane endeavors to mitigate the effects of loss of income due to unemployment, debilitating illness, or retirement. Last, the increasing costs of the burgeoning technologies of the personal health services spurred the creation of private and public health insurance.

The personal health services of the liberal democracies discussed here went through three stages of evolution: (1) the creation of the health services infrastructure; (2) the emergence of the third party for health insurance; and (3) the current stage of management and control. The last stage emerged because the costs of personal health services were pressing disproportionately on the allocation of funds to other goods and services.

The style of personal health services changed from one that was grossly holistic in the approach of the physician to the patient to an increasingly refined, reductionist identification of specific diseases, specific causes, and specific therapies. The reductionist approach became more effective and more and more expensive, and both the medical profession and the public accepted and bought it. Now, however, we are wondering how to manage multiple chronic illnesses in an aging population. These comments apply to all developed countries, where growing egalitarian values also powered the emergence of universal health insurance through the political process and the mandating of funding from public treasuries and employer and employee contributions.

The data for an understanding of the internal operations, the "black box" of decision making and resource allocation, are too fragmentary and frequently not comparable enough for a definitive work on cross-national comparisons. In fact, even if there were sufficient data, it is unlikely that there are enough distinctive national health services delivery systems in the world to formulate laws of development and criteria for judging systems "good" or "bad." So, methodologically, I have limited myself to seven impressionistically selected countries for a rather high level of abstraction from which to make general observations as to the nature of health services delivery systems in all developed countries.

The scientific, reductionist approach to disease and its diagnosis and therapy resulted in the creation in all countries of quite similar types of facilities—called general hospitals—and personnel: physicians, specialists, dentists, nurses, pharmacists, and, eventually, a host of specialized laboratory technicians. Facilities and services on the periphery are mental hospitals and nursing homes, which are difficult to meld into the reductionist model and must be managed holistically and custodially.

These similar types of facilities and personnel were, however, organized in a variety of delivery systems as products of historical, economic, social, and political circumstances. The United Kingdom, for example, developed a three-class hospital service structure with the famous voluntary hospitals accorded the most prestige because of their upper-class sponsorship of the working poor. The physicians who were selected to practice in them also became prestigious and served the upper class for a fee in private beds and private offices. The physicians who did not get admission privileges became general practitioners. In the United States, the voluntary hospitals were capitalized by private philanthropy and became the service institutions for the rapidly growing, broad middle- and upper-income groups with discretionary income; the poor, being proportionately fewer than in Europe, became a residual group.

Ownership of hospital facilities continues to be a mixture of private and public, even under universal health insurance. Governments contract with hospitals for mandated services, even, in the United Kingdom, with private hospitals for special services the National Health Service may not have. Methods of hospital reimbursement range from centrally determined budgets to global budgets for individual hospitals or, as in the United States, predetermined budgets for clusters of more or less related diagnoses. The trend is toward relatively arbitrary budget caps.

Physicians continue to be paid by the classic methods of fee-for-service, capitation (a sum per patient on their panels), and salary, but in varying proportions. Hospital-based physicians are more likely to be paid a salary than physicians not in hospitals, who receive a fee-for-service, a capitation payment, or both. Still, private patients pay their hospital-based physicians on a fee-for-service basis. No system proscribes private practice, and countries vary in the extent of private practice privileges.

In the liberal-democratic countries, physicians (except public health officers) are not regarded as employees of the government in a civil-service sense. They have managed to salvage a great deal of the liberal tradition of a free and autonomous profession. Physicians based in hospitals are analogous to tenured professors in universities. They work at rather than for the government. Granted, the government is a monopoly purchaser, so the physicians have little choice, but the legal position persists. So far, this observation does not hold for the United States.

To the extent that this liberal tradition of professional autonomy has been eroded, the countervailing action on the part of the profession is to stage work actions by slowdown or by simply walking off the job, leaving at most a skeleton staff to handle acute emergencies. The same is true for nurses. (Dentists apparently have not engaged in work actions because the public does not regard their services as an acute need.) So far, it seems, the profession has retained the professional prerogatives of determining diagnosis and treatment, at least within the resources provided to them. It is reasonable, however, that before long physicians may strike because of insufficient resources for good quality service.

The health services systems vary as to the number of entry points at which patients can get into the system for nonemergent causes, ranging from several, as is true in most countries, to one, as in the United Kingdom. There seems, however, to be an implicit desire if not an explicit policy to have one entry point, in the form of a primary care physician, who can perform triage and refer patients to specialists as indicated. Medical authorities and administrators regard one entry point as more efficient and possibly less costly, and whether or not systems are deliberately structured with physician gatekeepers, individuals and families by custom tend to have a physician. There are few data on this, but a 1982 report on a sampling of the adult Swedish population reported 48.5 percent had a regular physician, whereas in the United States 85 percent so reported. In the United Kingdom, 95 percent or so of the population have a regular primary physician because the system can only be entered through the primary physician.[1] No matter what the restrictions on entry, all systems subscribe to the desirability of free choice of physician, to enhance the physician-patient relationship.

For both hospitals and physicians—as well as for other health services personnel—methods and amounts of payment are constantly problematic. Neither amounts nor even methods—which would seem to be a mechanical administrative matter—really stabilize over the long run.

Given the reasonable assumption that developed countries with relatively high standards of living would have somewhat similar mortality and morbidity patterns, it seems remarkable that there are such great variations in the supply of hospital beds and in supply of physicians, dentists, and other types of personnel. Apparently, the reciprocal response between supply and need or supply and demand can operationally be a highly varied one. There is a great deal of variance among populations as to what is a tolerable balance between need or demand and the supply of facilities and personnel, as described in Chapter 9.

In all countries, among planners and big buyers of services, the desired model for health services delivery includes salaried positions for both hospital-based specialists and general practitioners as well as primary physicians in group practices or clinics outside the hospital. There seems to be a desire for patients to have only one entry point, the primary physician, who is supposed to be the medical counselor for the individual and the family and who will refer patients to hospital-based specialists as needed. The general public is not sufficiently knowledgeable to select specialists directly. Even in the United States, the group practice medical plans (health maintenance organizations) seem to structure access to their services through a primary physician.

Is there then a more or less standard model of health services delivery system appearing in all developed countries caused by the same forces to contain costs and rationalize the system? The trends are there, but the possibility of their evolving to a logical conclusion that will satisfy the desires of administrators and planners still appears to be quite murky. Given the current—and future—state of the art of setting up and operating health services delivery systems, a single model does not seem to be practical. There are too many forces outside of the technocratic medical model that shape organizational structure: the perceptions of physicians, the need or demand perceptions of patients, the sources and amounts of funding (private and public), and the dynamics of medical technology, of which there seems to be no end. The one constant, even in the United States, is the drive for universal health insurance so that no one suffers unbearable costs because of illness. Delivery structure and sources of funding can vary considerably after universality has been assured.

As a final observation, I and others have expressed the simple truism that a health services delivery system is shaped by and is a product of a combination of economic, social, and political circumstances and is thus, so to speak, a dependent variable of powerful external forces. This accounts for the variations of organizational structures described in this book.

Perhaps the time has come to question the conventional wisdom of this quite reasonable generalization. The effects of an aging population on the health and caring services, the ability of high technology medicine to prolong life even in a vegetable state, the crush of expensive technology on priorities for other goods and services, and so on and on, may turn out to be powerful forces that will affect consumer behavior and cause us to reevaluate both the meaning of dying and the worth of the individual against the needs of society as a whole. If present trends continue, the health services enterprise will dominate all aspects of society in a manner analogous to the role of the medieval church—except that the health services cathedrals will be temples to the body replacing temples to the soul.

Note

1. Sjukvårdens och Socialvårdens Planerings-och Rationaliseringsinstitut (SPRI), *Hur Mår Du Sverige?* (Stockholm: SPRI, 1982), p. 68.

Index

About the Author

ODIN W. ANDERSON is Professor of Sociology on the faculties of the University of Chicago, Graduate Program in Health Administration, Graduate School of Business, and University of Wisconsin, Department of Sociology and the Program in Health Services Administration. He was Director, at Chicago, of both the program and The Center for Health Administration Studies. Earlier in his career he taught at The University of Western Ontario, New York University, and Columbia University. Dr. Anderson earned his Ph.D. at The University of Michigan in Sociology. He is a Fellow of the American Sociological Association, the American Public Health Association, the American Association for the Advancement of Science, and the Institute of Medicine, and an Honorary Fellow of the American College of Healthcare Executives. He has an Honorary Doctorate (Faculty of Medicine) from Uppsala University, Uppsala, Sweden. Dr. Anderson has published many books and journal articles.